PR 3009 .R72 19
Root, Robert K.
Classical mythology in
Shakespeare.

W9-BWF-113

YALE STUDIES IN ENGLISH

ALBERT S. COOK, EDITOR

XIX

CLASSICAL MYTHOLOGY

IN SHAKESPEARE

BY

ROBERT KILBURN ROOT, PH.D.

Instructor in English in Yale University

A Thesis presented to the Philosophical Faculty of Yale University
in Candidacy for the Degree of
Doctor of Philosophy

NEW YORK
GORDIAN PRESS, INC.
1965

CITY COLLEGE LIBRARY
1825 MAY ST.
BROWNSVILLE, TEXAS 78520

Originally Published 1903
Reprinted 1965

Library of Congress Catalog Card No. 65-24996

Printed in U.S.A. by
EDWARDS BROTHERS, INC.
Ann Arbor, Michigan

PR
3009
.R72

TO

PROFESSOR ALBERT S. COOK

IN GRATEFUL ACKNOWLEDGMENT OF HIS GENEROUS HELP

PREFACE

The term classical mythology has been taken to include not only the divinities of the ancient religion and such tales as those of Ovid's *Metamorphoses,* but also the heroes of the Trojan war and the personages of the *Æneid.* In a number of cases, such, for example, as Fortune, Nature, and Fame, it has not been easy to draw a hard and fast line between mythology and mere philosophical personification. In Part First, where the myths are discussed severally, I have been inclined to include such subjects, while excluding them as doubtful from the generalizations of Part Second and the Introduction.

Any work in the field of Shakespearian commentary must, of course, be a gleaning of the ears left unnoticed by earlier commentators; but in my corner of the field I have found the gleaning richer than I expected. Though the great mass of Shakespearian scholarship makes it impossible to say with certainty that any given point has not been noticed, I have found that after free use of the Variorum edition of 1821 and, as far as it has been completed, of the Variorum edition of Dr. Furness, there was still plenty of room for original investigation. In this investigation the mythological dictionaries of Roscher, Pauly-Wissowa, and Smith have been of constant assistance. The Globe edition of Shakespeare has been used for quotation and reference; but in giving a list of citations I have followed the approximately chronological order of the plays in the Leopold edition, though always putting the doubtful plays at the end of the list. In citing Shakespearian plays, I have adopted the abbreviations of Schmidt's Shakespeare Lexicon. The citations from Golding's Ovid are from the edition of 1575. The editions of Ovid and Vergil by Merkel and Ribbeck respectively have been used in citations from those authors.

July 21, 1903.

INTRODUCTION

I

Every student of European culture is compelled, sooner
or later, to attempt a definition of those complex and inter-
woven, yet none the less clearly divergent, tendencies which
we call Mediævalism and the Renaissance. All definition is
a perilous undertaking: one constructs his laborious formula
only to be greeted with the mocking laugh of some forgotten
aspect; and the definition must be begun anew. Especially
is this true in the particular problem of definition I have
suggested: if one bases his definition of Mediævalism on
Dante and the cathedral-builders, how is he to include the
contradictory phenomenon of the French fabliau, and its
satyr train of goliards and jongleurs? The maker of
definitions is sure to find his course bound in shallows and
in miseries until he recognizes that the terms Mediævalism
and Renaissance do not stand so much for two periods of
history as for two tendencies, two hostile forces, which in
half-hearted truce or open warfare have always coexisted,
and must always coexist, in the heart of man, and consequently in his literature and art. In the thirteenth century
Mediævalism had the upper hand; in the sixteenth, its
enemy insulted over it. Without risking an inclusive definition, one may say that Mediæval art has its gaze fixed
primarily on the spiritual, that of the Renaissance on the
sensuous. Mediævalism proclaims that the eternal things
of the spirit are alone worth while; the Renaissance declares
that man's life consists, if not in the abundance of the
things he possesses, at any rate in the abundance and variety
of the sensations he enjoys.

When Petrarch and the scholars of the succeeding genera-
tions rediscovered the half-forgotten monuments of classical
antiquity, they seemed to find authority for this rich life of

the senses; in the mythology of the ancients, as it glows resplendent in the pages of Ovid, they found the *Credo* and the *Gloria in Excelsis* of the new life. Could they have lighted first on Homer and Pindar and the Attic Three, things might have been different; but it was Ovid, the brilliant, the sensuous, least spiritual of the ancients, who became the poet's poet, the painter's poet, the dominant influence in the art of the Renaissance. It is the mythology of Ovid that crowds the pages of Boccaccio and Chaucer; it is the divinities of Ovid that elbow the virgins and saints in every picture-gallery of Europe; it was to Ovid that Shakespeare, called of some the 'child of the Renaissance,' turned for the classical allusions which the taste of the sixteenth century demanded in its literature.

It has been the aim of the present study to collect and examine systematically the very numerous allusions to classical mythology in the authentic works of Shakespeare, with the purpose of determining the sources from which he drew his acquaintance with the matter, the conception which he entertained of it, and the extent to which it became a vital element in his art. It is the purpose of this introduction to summarize the more important results of the study, and to frame certain generalizations on the basis of the facts detailed in the pages which follow.

In considering the problem of sources, it is necessary to distinguish first of all between the definite, detailed allusions, such as imply a more or less accurate acquaintance with the myth alluded to, and the vaguer, more general allusions, such as might be made by any fairly intelligent man, though he had never read a line of the classics. For example, a mere mention of the labors of Hercules indicates no real acquaintance with classic myth; but an allusion to the death of Hercules with mention of the poisoned shirt of Nessus and the fate of the page Lichas, lodged by his master on the horns of the moon,[1] is possible only to one who has read

---

[1] Ant. 4. 12. 43-5.

a detailed account of the fable, such as that given by Ovid or Seneca. Though the number of these definite allusions in Shakespeare is smaller than that of the vague ones, they are yet sufficiently numerous to admit of satisfactory conclusions. Of these allusions for which a definite source can be assigned, it will be found that an overwhelming majority are directly due to Ovid, while the remainder, with few exceptions, are from Vergil. The vaguer allusions, though admitting of no confident attribution, are nearly all of such a character that they *might* have been drawn from Ovid or Vergil. In other words, a man familiar with these two authors, and with no others, would be able to make all the mythological allusions contained in the undisputed works of Shakespeare, barring some few exceptions to be considered later. Throughout, the influence of Ovid is at least four times as great as that of Vergil; the whole character of Shakespeare's mythology is essentially Ovidian.

Of the particular poems of Ovid, it is but natural that the *Metamorphoses* should furnish Shakespeare with the bulk of his mythology. With nearly all of the important episodes of the poem, with each of the fifteen books, save perhaps the twelfth and fifteenth, his familiarity is clearly demonstrable. The highly dramatic quality of the *Heroides* must surely have made them congenial reading, and allusions to the myth of Ariadne, to Leda, and to the dream of Hecuba that she had brought forth a firebrand, indicate that the work was not unfamiliar. In the *Taming of the Shrew* there is even a direct Latin quotation from the first epistle;[1] but the uncertain extent of Shakespeare's authorship in this play makes the bit of evidence less conclusive. From the *Fasti* Shakespeare certainly drew much of his *Rape of Lucrece*,[2] and to the same work is probably to be referred an allusion to Arion on the dolphin's back in *Twelfth Night*. From the *Amores* is taken the Latin motto

---

[1] Shr. 3. 1. 28-9. Cf. *Her.* 1. 33-4.

[2] I had reached this conclusion independently before reading the convincing examination of the sources of the poem by Wilhelm Ewig in *Angl.* 22.

prefixed to *Venus and Adonis;* while the *Ars Amatoria* may explain Shakespeare's acquaintance with the intrigue of Mars and Venus, and Juliet's statement: 'At lovers' perjuries, they say, Jove laughs.'[1]   The only positive evidence of indebtedness to the *Tristia* is found in a mention of Medea and Absyrtus in the doubtfully authentic *II Henry VI.*

Sharply contrasted with the frequency and variety of Shakespeare's references to Ovid is the comparative paucity and narrow scope of his Vergilian allusion. Perhaps the restraint and delicacy of Vergil's art are less in harmony with the temper of the Elizabethan age; perhaps his story lends itself less readily to casual allusion. Only three episodes of the *Æneid* seem to have made a deep impression on Shakespeare—the account of the fall of Troy with the stratagem of Sinon and the death of Priam, the grief of the forsaken Dido, and the infernal machinery of Vergil's Hades—episodes all of them which savor more or less of the sensational, and thus approach the prevailing taste of Shakespeare's day. Shakespeare is not content, however, with merely selecting sensational episodes; he sets to work deliberately to heighten the sensationalism. The truth of this statement is at once apparent if one compares the account of Priam's death in the player's speech in *Hamlet* with the lines of the second book of the *Æneid* on which it is founded;[2] but since Shakespeare's authorship of these lines has been disputed, it may be proved by an equally characteristic example from the *Merchant of Venice.* Lorenzo says:

> The moon shines bright . . . . . .
> . . . . In such a night
> Stood Dido with a willow in her hand
> Upon the wild sea banks, and waft her love
> To come again to Carthage.[3]

[1] Rom. 2. 2. 92-3. Cf. *Art.* 1. 633, but see s. v. Jupiter. As bearing on Shakespeare's acquaintance with the poem, compare Lucentio's words in Shr. 4. 2. 8: 'I read that I profess, the Art to Love.'

[2] Cf. *infra* s. v. Priam.

[3] Merch. 5. 1. 9-12.

Vergil's Dido is left disconsolate at Carthage; but for this particular scene the *Æneid* may be searched in vain. So essentially un-Vergilian is it, that Matthew Arnold quotes the lines in his *Essay on Celtic Literature* as an example of what he is pleased to call 'natural magic,' and which he attributes to the Celtic influence on English literature. One need not, however, go to the Celts for this particular passage: it is closely imitated from the tenth epistle of Ovid's *Heroides,* where Ariadne, discovering the flight of Theseus, goes down by moonlight to the wild rocky shore of her island, and after calling in vain for her love, binds her white veil to a long wand, and waves it above her head, that 'though he hear not, he may at least perceive her with his eyes.' Chaucer has adapted these lines in his legend of Ariadne,[1] and it is of course possible that Shakespeare read them there; but wherever read, they appealed to him as Ovid always appealed. The' instance is a striking illustration of the essentially Ovidian character of Shakespeare's mythology.

Of Latin influence other than that of Ovid and Vergil there is very little trace. It might have been expected that the dramas of Seneca, dealing, many of them, with mythological subjects, and teeming with mythological allusion, would be found responsible for some of Shakespeare's references; for they were popular in the Elizabethan era, and available in English translation. But of such influence I have discovered but two possible instances, neither of which is conclusive.[2] Now and then, too, one is tempted to discover a trace of Horace or Martial; but the instances are very rare and far from convincing.

But what part do the Greek poets play? Shakespeare has left no sonnet to tell us how he felt on first looking into Chapman's Homer; but that he did look into it is proved by the fact that several incidents in *Troilus and Cressida* are founded on the *Iliad*, and that in three or four instances

---

[1] *Legend of Good Women* 1185 ff.

[2] Cf. *infra*, s. v. Hercules. See also Cunliffe, *The Influence of Seneca on Elizabethan Tragedy,* London, 1893.

a mythological allusion must be referred to the same source.[1] That he found in it no undiscovered sea of thought, that its influence on his conception of classical mythology was all but nothing, the exceeding paucity of such allusions abundantly indicates. Of any other Greek influence there is not the slightest hint. Mr. John Churton Collins, in a series of articles in the *Fortnightly* for 1903, has tried to show that Shakespeare was familiar with the Greek dramatists in Latin translation. At the time of going to press, the last article of his series has not yet appeared; but in the articles already published I find no evidence sufficient to overthrow my own belief that he was totally unacquainted with them. It is at any rate certain that he no where alludes to any of the characters or episodes of the Greek drama, that they exerted no influence whatever on his conception of mythology.[2] The all but total disregard of the genealogies and family relationships of the divinities, which appear so prominently in Spenser and Milton, shows that Shakespeare could not have been familiar with Hesiod.

I do not propose to enter the lists of those who since the days of Farmer have disputed back and forth whether or not Shakespeare was able to read Ovid and Vergil in the original Latin.[3] A number of verbal correspondences between Shakespeare and Golding's Ovid have been noticed by the critics, and my own studies have added materially to the list.[4] That he was familiar with this excellent version of the *Metamorphoses* is beyond question: but that he also read the poem in the original is in the highest degree prob-

[1] Cf. *infra* s. v. Mars.

[2] Further on I shall notice instances of such allusion in Tit., which I do not regard as Shakespeare's.

[3] An admirable summary of the arguments is given by Mr. J. Churton Collins in the articles referred to above. See also the articles by Professor Baynes called *What Shakespeare Learned at School, Fraser's Magazine,* New Series, Vol. 21.

[4] Instances of such correspondence more or less convincing are noticed frequently in the pages which follow. See for examples s. v. Actæon, Adonis, Argonauts, Cimmerian, Diana (Hecate), Hiems, Jupiter, Phaeton, Proteus.

able. As regards Vergil, I have found one passage that
seems to indicate acquaintance with the translation of Phaer,[1]
and another in which the original must have been consulted.[2]
After all, the important point for this investigation is that
Shakespeare knew Ovid and Vergil, not that he read them
in this language or that.[3]

It may be objected, however, that the stories of Vergil
and Ovid are common property, that they appear in countless
reworkings and paraphrases—in Chaucer, in Gower, in
Spenser. Could not Shakespeare have learned his mythology entirely at second-hand from English authors? That
in certain instances his acquaintance with a particular myth
was acquired in this way is more than probable, and in the
following pages I have frequently suggested an indebtedness of this sort; but that the whole, or even the main part,
of his mythology was so acquired is utterly improbable. It
must be remembered that we have the most complete evidence that Shakespeare was intimately familiar with the
Metamorphoses in Golding's version. It is equally certain
that in composing his *Rape of Lucrece* the poet had recourse
to Ovid's *Fasti* and to Livy, as well as to Chaucer, and per-

---

[1] Cf. s. v. Iris.   [2] Cf. s. v. Sinon.

[3] An examination of the articles dealing with the several myths
will show that Shakespeare's knowledge of the myths, though frequently scanty, is in general substantially correct. Only four instances
of actual error have come to my notice: the confusion about Althæa's
firebrand in H4B 2. 2. 93, 95; the idea that Cerberus was killed by
Hercules expressed in LLL 5. 2. 593; the use of the word 'Hesperides' as the name of the garden where grew the golden apples,
with the idea that Hercules gathered the apples himself, LLL 4. 3.
341; Per. 1. 1. 27; Cor. 4. 6. 99; and the famous mention of Juno's
swans in As 1. 3. 77. To this list may be added the mistaken form
'Ariachne' of Troil. 5. 2. 152, and the somewhat confused notions
entertained of Lethe and Acheron. Other errors, such as making
Delphi an island, Wint. 3. 1. 2; considering the sun as Aurora's
lover; and thinking of Perseus as mounted on the winged steed
Pegasus, are hardly to be laid to Shakespeare's account, since they
are all shared by his contemporaries.

haps Gower.[1]   It is, moreover, inherently so improbable that Shakespeare, with his quick and eager intelligence, should have been content to rest ignorant of Ovid and Vergil, that the burden of proof may fairly be left with those who may choose to assert his ignorance.[2]

II

If, then, Shakespeare learned his mythology mainly from Ovid, what conception did he entertain of it?   He found in Ovid, and in classical mythology as a whole, what all the Renaissance found before him: a treasure-house of fascinating story wrought out in rich magnificence of detail, all but void of any deep spiritual significance.   Graceful ornament and brilliant imagery he found in abundance; but for the expression of his profound meditations on the great mysteries which round our little life he found small aid.   In so far as Shakespeare is a 'child of the Renaissance,' a reveler in the beauty of external form, he finds Ovid congenial reading; in so far as he represents the deeper spirit which I have called Mediævalism, he finds Ovid, and the system he learned from Ovid, quite inadequate.   Shakespeare is essentially religious; Ovid is as essentially irreligious.[3]

That this assertion is no mere *a priori* inference may easily be shown by an analysis of the mythological allusions in a few representative plays.   I shall first show that even in his earlier period, when the influence of Ovid was strongest upon him, Shakespeare felt that mythological allusion was out of keeping with the highest seriousness of thought and passion; and, secondly, that his attitude toward mythology

[1] See the work of Wilhelm Ewig in *Angl.* 22, referred to above.

[2] Caxton's *Recuyell,* though it furnished Shakespeare with many hints for his *Troilus and Cressida,* has not, so far as I can discover, supplied him with material for a single allusion.

[3] For an able exposition of the way in which under different conditions a modern poet has made classical mythology subservient to the expression of deep religious truth, see *The Classical Mythology of Milton's English Poems,* by C. G. Osgood, New York, 1900.

underwent a steady development as his life advanced. The first point may be quickly proved from *Merchant of Venice* and *Romeo and Juliet.* Though the first of these plays abounds in mythological allusions, not a single instance of such allusion is to be found in the great trial scene of Act IV. Of the 25 mythological allusions in *Romeo and Juliet,* all but 5 occur in the first two acts; 4 are in Act III, leaving one allusion to be spoken by the courtly Paris in Act IV, and none at all for Act V. As the tragedy darkens, as the seriousness deepens, mythology weakens and disappears. From *Hamlet,* too, may be drawn further corroboration of this tendency. Hamlet as a student of the university, a scholar and thinker, alludes fourteen times to classic myth: when he wishes to dilate on the excellencies of his dead father, he is ready with comparisons to the curls of Hyperion, to the front of Jove, the 'station of the herald Mercury'; his mother of a month ago, weeping over her dead husband, he scornfully compares to Niobe, all tears; he fears that the spirit which appeared to him may have been a damned ghost, and his own imaginations 'as foul as Vulcan's stithy.' But it is immediately noticeable that in his deeper, more serious speeches, these allusions do not occur, and that in the more harrowing scenes of the last two acts they all but wholly cease.

If the Ovidian mythology is excluded from the more serious portions of *Romeo and Juliet* and the *Merchant of Venice,* we should expect to find its influence steadily diminishing as Shakespeare's art becomes more profound; and this is indeed the case, but the change is too significant to be dismissed with a mere statement. In the dedication to the first edition of *Venus and Adonis* (1593), Shakespeare describes it as the first heir of his invention; and though these words may not justify us in considering the poem absolutely the first of his ventures, we are none the less safe in placing it among the earliest of his works. Founded on two Ovidian myths, that of Adonis and that of Salmacis, the poem is in subject-matter and treatment the most

essentially Ovidian of Shakespeare's works.   In the dramas,
however, Ovid's influence is more marked a little later.   In
the earliest of the plays, such as *Comedy of Errors, Two
Gentlemen of Verona,* and the first of the histories, the number of allusions is never more than six or eight.[1]   It is in
the *Merchant of Venice* that Ovidian allusion is most happily
employed.   Of the 28 allusions, 13 are detailed, and several
are highly elaborate.   Of the detailed allusions, 10 are
to Ovidian story, and embrace such subjects as Orpheus,
Midas, Argus, Thisbe, the rescue of Hesione, Hercules and
his page Lichas; to the story of Medea and Jason there are
three separate allusions.   It is to be noticed, however, that
the divinities are seldom referred to.   The spirit in which
mythology is employed is best exhibited by quoting the
familiar lines which open the fifth act:

> *Lor.*   The moon shines bright: in such a night as this,
>   When the sweet wind did gently kiss the trees
>   And they did make no noise, in such a night
>   Troilus methinks mounted the Troyan walls
>   And sigh'd his soul toward the Grecian tents,
>   Where Cressid lay that night.
> *Jes.*   In such a night
>   Did Thisbe fearfully o'ertrip the dew
>   And saw the lion's shadow ere himself
>   And ran dismayed away.
> *Lor.*   In such a night
>   Stood Dido with a willow in her hand
>   Upon the wild sea banks and waft her love
>   To come again to Carthage.
> *Jes.*   In such a night
>   Medea gather'd the enchanted herbs
>   That did renew old Æson.

It is in such graceful and altogether charming embellish-
ment that the classical mythology appears in the earlier
plays.

[1] *Love's Labor's Lost* is an exception to this statement; but I am
inclined to think that the abundance of allusion in this play is due
to the revision which it received in 1598, and is therefore to be
assigned to the later period.

I cannot better show the change which now comes over the spirit of this classical allusion than by quoting in close proximity to these lines the following speech of Rosalind in *As You Like It:*

No, faith, die by attorney. The poor world is almost six thousand years old, and in all this time there was not any man died in his own person, videlicet, in a love-cause. Troilus had his brains dashed out with a Grecian club; yet he did what he could to die before, and he is one of the patterns of love. Leander, he would have lived many a fair year, though Hero had turned nun, if it had not been for a hot midsummer night; for, good youth, he went but forth to wash him in the Hellespont and being taken with a cramp was drowned: and the foolish chroniclers of that age found it was 'Hero of Sestos.' But these are all lies: men have died from time to time and worms have eaten them, but not for love.[1]

Instead of graceful, serious allusion, we have delicate raillery; to the clear common-sense of Rosalind the heroes of the mythographers are but an idle jest. Nor is Rosalind peculiar in this attitude; Celia, Touchstone, and Jaques all furnish examples of the same treatment. When we add that in *II Henry IV*, the *Merry Wives*, and *Much Ado*, written all of them at about the same time as *As You Like It*, the mythological allusions are of the same character, or even more broadly humorous, that of the 30 allusions in *Much Ado* 25 are playful or scoffing, we are safe in affirming that Shakespeare's attitude has changed, that he has recognized the insincerity of the Ovidian system, and finds in it only the material for a jest. I would not be understood to say that this change is either sudden or complete. Even in the *Merchant of Venice* may be found three instances of humorous allusion in the speeches of Launcelot Gobbo, and in *Midsummer Night's Dream* we have the delicious burlesque of an Ovidian story in the play of the mechanicals; while there are still several instances of the graceful, serious allusion in *As You Like It* and *Twelfth Night*. But the relative proportion of the serious anl playful allusions in the plays of the two periods has been startlingly reversed:

[1] As 4. 1. 94-108.

in the *Merchant of Venice* there are 3 playful allusions to 25 serious, in *Much Ado* 5 serious to 25 playful.

Having first turned the myths of Ovid into a jest, Shakespeare's next step was to exclude them in large measure from his plays. In *Hamlet* they are retained, as I noticed earlier, to indicate the academic tendencies of Hamlet's thought—though to be sure it is Vergil rather than the less serious Ovid who seems to be most in Shakespeare's mind; but in *Julius Cæsar,* written in 1601, there are but 5 allusions, none of them Ovidian: in *Measure for Measure* there are but 2, in *Othello* 11, in *Macbeth* 8, in *Lear* but 5. When these numbers are compared with those given for the earlier plays, their significance is apparent. Equally significant is the character of the few allusions which remain. Here we find neither the graceful ornament of the earlier dramas nor the playful humor of the period which follows; we find rather a groping after the deeper meaning of the myth. Of the 8 allusions in *Macbeth,* for example, all but one are to the more terrible or destructive aspects of ancient religion: Hecate appears on the stage as queen of the witches, and Macbeth makes two independent allusions to her as the spirit of darkness, while Acheron, the Gorgon, and perhaps the Harpies, complete the mythology of horror. In *Othello,* 6 of the 11 allusions are spoken by Othello himself. These have to do with the larger, grander conceptions of mythology—with Olympus, Jove the thunderer, Diana as a type of chastity, the prophetic fury of the Sibyl, Promethean fire. Especially characteristic of Othello's mythology are the lines in which he meditates the death of Desdemona:

> But once put out thy light,
> Thou cunning'st pattern of excelling nature,
> I know not where is that Promethean heat
> That can thy light relume.[1]

Iago employs mythology in a way equally accordant with his character: a conventional allusion to his muse, a dis-

[1] Oth. 5. 2. 10-13.

agreeable reference to the erotic myths about that Jove whom
Othello thinks of as thunderer, and an oath by the double-
faced Janus.[1]

It is this striving after a deeper meaning or greater appropriateness which marks the allusions in the plays of the
latest period. The number of allusions is as great as in the
plays of the earlier period, and the substance of them is
still to be attributed to Ovid or Vergil, but instead of the
fables of Ovid we find rather his divinities, standing as
types of the great forces of nature or of the great moral
forces in the life of man. Of this usage *Cymbeline* may
be taken to furnish the type. If we exclude from consideration the elaborate masque in Act V, the authenticity of which
has been doubted, and also the incidental references to Jove
which merely mark the pagan background of the play, we
find 31 mythological allusions. Of these about 75 per cent.
have to do with the greater divinities, while Ovidian allusion
in the narrower sense consists of single references to the
tale of Tereus, and to the death of Hecuba (from the thirteenth book of the *Metamorphoses*). Diana appears three
times as patroness of chastity, and twice as huntress;
Phœbus or Titan is three times mentioned as sun-god; and
nature-myth appears also in references to Night with her
dragon-yoke, and to Neptune. Venus is mentioned as a
type of beauty; and Mercury, Mars, Jove, and Minerva also
furnish types of physical excellence. From the Troy-story
we have Æneas and Sinon as types of falseness, Ajax as
a type of strength, and Thersites of base cowardice. In
general, then, the myths appear not in explicit allusion, but
as types of qualities, physical or moral.[2]

[1] See also Lear's words to Cordelia, Lr. 4. 7. 45-8, quoted below.

[2] One may notice that, of the divinities, Cupid is mentioned but 5
times after 1601.

III

I have tried to establish two main points: first, that with few exceptions Shakespeare's allusions to classical mythology have to do with myths, the substance of which may be found in Ovid or Vergil; secondly, that his employment of these allusions is clearly different at different periods of his work. If these conclusions are accepted, we gain from the first a new sort of internal evidence as to the Shakespearian authorship of a disputed play or portion of a play; from the second a new sort of internal evidence for determining the date of composition of a play known to be Shakespeare's. I shall now consider these tests in some detail.

Before applying the test of authenticity to any definite case, it must be clearly understood what the test is capable of proving, and what it cannot prove. Though it may offer corroborative evidence, it cannot prove Shakespeare's authorship of any play or portion of a play. If the mythological allusions in a disputed play agree never so closely in matter and in manner with those in the poet's undisputed works, the most that we can affirm is that Shakespeare may have been its author. Thus, for example, it has long been subject of dispute to what extent Shakespeare is responsible for the *Taming of the Shrew*. An examination of the mythology of the play shows 13 allusions, of which 9 are to be traced to Ovid, 1 to Vergil, while 3 are too vague to admit of attribution. There is no allusion which Shakespeare might not have made, and the character of the allusions is such as we should expect in a Shakespearian play written at about the same time as the *Merchant of Venice*. In the case of this play, then, the test proves that Shakespeare may have written the whole play; it lends indeed some probability to such an ascription; but it is totally unable to prove that he did write it. If, on the other hand, a play contains allusions to myths which are never referred to in the unquestioned plays, the knowledge of which could only have been acquired from authors to whom Shakespeare is never indebted, the assumption is strong that the play in question is not his work. This may best be illustrated from *Titus Andronicus,* the Shakespearian authorship of which has long been doubted.[1]

One is first of all impressed by the extraordinary number of the allusions. There are 53 in all, a number equaled among Shakespeare's authentic plays only in *Troilus and Cressida,* which belongs to a much later period, and in sharp contrast to the 6 references of the *Comedy of Errors,* the 8 of *Two Gentlemen of Verona,* and the 5, 6, and 8 of the three earliest histories.[2] One is next impressed by the fact that a large proportion of the allusions are more definite and detailed than Shakespeare usually exhibits, almost giving the impression that the author had his Ovid or Vergil open before him as he wrote;[3] 14 of the references are clearly

[1] The present state of critical opinion is summed up as follows by Frederick Boas in *Shakespeare and his Predecessors,* 1899: 'The external evidence is entirely in favor of the play being by Shakespeare. It was included by Heminge and Condell in the first folio, and it is mentioned by Meres in 1598. It dates almost certainly from 1587 or 1588, for in the introduction to *Bartholomew Fair,* 1614, Ben Jonson declares that any man "who will swear *Jeronimo* or *Andronicus* are the best plays yet, shows that his judgment hath stood still these five and twenty or thirty years." Thus external evidence pronounces that *Titus Andronicus* was written by Shakespeare immediately after leaving Stratford, and the chief German critics (e. g. Kreyssig, Ulrici, and Hertzberg) accept this view. English commentators, however, almost without exception, have refused to recognize the play as genuinely Shakespearian, and have at most admitted that it was touched up by the poet. A stage tradition dating from 1687 affords slender support to this theory, which, otherwise, rests purely upon æsthetic considerations arising out of the nature of the plot and its treatment.'
Brandes accepts the play without reservation, Sidney Lee with some unwillingness.

[2] I have already had occasion to notice that most of the 38 allusions in *Love's Labor's Lost* are of a character to indicate that they belong to the revision which the play received in 1598.

[3] Perhaps, though, one should not lay undue weight on this point, since Shakespeare, if it was he who wrote the play, could not have been far advanced from his school-days.

due to Ovid, and 14 as clearly to the poet of Mantua. Of much more significance is the fact that the author of *Titus* seems in several instances to show an acquaintance with the Greek drama.[1]

Thus in 1. 1. 379-381 Marcus says:

> The Greeks upon advice did bury Ajax
> That slew himself; and wise Laertes' son
> Did graciously plead for his funerals.

Shakespeare's knowledge of Ajax, as displayed in the authentic plays, was obtained mainly from the account of his dispute with Ulysses over the arms of Achilles, given by Ovid in *Met.* 13. Though Caxton and Chapman's Homer furnished him with the main incidents of the action of Ajax in *Troilus and Cressida,* even here the character of the Telamonian hero is that given by Ovid;[2] and though Ajax is seven times mentioned outside of *Troilus,* only once does Shakespeare refer to any event connected with him which is not given by Ovid.[3] Where, then, did the author of *Titus* learn that the incensed Greeks were unwilling to grant burial to Ajax, until persuaded by the eloquence of his rival Ulysses? I can only say that the episode may easily be found in the *Ajax* of Sophocles,[4] but that I have looked in vain for any mention of the incident in other authors, Latin or English, whom Shakespeare may reasonably be supposed to have read. Similarly, there are two allusions in *Titus* to the madness of Hecuba which seem closer to the *Hecuba* of Euripides than to the account of Hecuba's madness given by Ovid.[5] Lastly, we have an allusion to Prometheus 'tied to Caucasus'; and though it would be unwise to assert from a reference to so familiar an idea

[1] Cf. *supra,* p. 6.

[2] See s. v. Ajax.

[3] The single exception is found in LLL 4. 3. 7, where there is a vague allusion to Ajax killing sheep in his madness, a detail which might have been learned from the *Satires* of Horace. Cf. s. v. Ajax.

[4] Ll. 1332 seq.

[5] See s. v. Hecuba.

that the author had read Æschylus, it is noteworthy that, in the authentic plays, Shakespeare knows of Prometheus only as the fashioner of the human race, breathing the fire of life into the images which he has formed. When one adds that in six passages of *Titus* are found mythological names which, though perfectly possible to Shakespeare, are as a matter of fact never mentioned in the authentic plays,[1] the evidence becomes strong that Shakespeare is not the author.[2]

It is with a somewhat less assertive confidence that I advance my second theory, that the mythological allusions in an accepted play of Shakespeare furnish internal evidence for determining its date of composition. Internal evidence in these questions is always a matter deep and dangerous, for it presupposes that the sacred river of your author's intellectual and spiritual progress flows steadily onward, with no sudden rapids or capricious backward swirls; it assumes rather presumptuously that the caverns through which it runs *are* measurable to man after all. Still, if I am right in the analysis I have made of Shakespeare's attitude toward mythology at different periods of his work, it ought to be possible to say with some plausibility to what period a given play belongs.

None of Shakespeare's plays has offered more baffling problems to the chronologist than *Troilus and Cressida.* Furnivall placed it near the end of what he calls the poet's third period, just before *Antony and Cleopatra.* Fleay, on the other hand, assigned a portion of it (i. e. the Troilus story) to about 1594, and declared that it was completed by another hand in 1599, revised in 1602, and finally rewritten by Shakespeare in 1605.[3] More recent authorities are

---

[1] Astræa, the Cimmerians, Cocytus, Enceladus, the House of Fame, Pallas. Astræa is also mentioned in H6A 1. 6. 4.

[2] See also the discussion of the mythology of the three parts of *Henry VI* on p. 133.

[3] Fleay is fond of such elaborate dismemberments. I may add that I have examined separately the mythology of the several portions into which he divides the play, and fail to find the slightest support for his hypothesis.

2

CITY COLLEGE LIBRARY
1825 MAY ST.
BROWNSVILLE, TEXAS 78520

inclined to place it in 1601-1602.[1] I shall not attempt to
go into a discussion of the arguments, but shall merely
analyze the mythology of the play, and consider the evidence
furnished by it to the question of chronology.

To begin with, the number of allusions is much larger
than in any other play. Not only is the whole drama based
directly on the incidents of the Troy-myth as found in
Homer, Chaucer, and Caxton, but in the course of the
dialogue the other myths of classical antiquity are referred
to with remarkable frequency. If we exclude from consideration frequent oaths by Jove introduced to indicate the
pagan setting of the play, we find no less than 56 instances
of mythological allusion—half as many again as in *Antony
and Cleopatra,* which shows the next largest number.
Nature-myth occurs 11 times, always with strict metonymy;
Cupid is mentioned 6 times in a half playful, half serious
way; and the other divinities appear 28 times. There are
10 allusions to Ovidian fable—Arachne, Argus, Apollo and
Daphne, Jupiter and Europa, Mars and Venus, Niobe,
Perseus (twice), Typhon, Cerberus, and Proserpina. Of
Vergilian origin are references to Charon, Styx, and the
Elysian Fields; while to Chapman's Homer may be referred
an allusion to the combat of Mars and Diomed. Sixteen
of the allusions are humorous.

If we ask, now, to which of Shakespeare's periods such a
treatment of mythology belongs, we find that it belongs to
none of his periods, that it seems to combine the manners
of two periods: that of *Much Ado* and *As You Like It,*
with that of *Antony and Cleopatra* and *Coriolanus.* The
many proofs of Ovidian influence, the frequent mentions of
Cupid and Venus, and still more strongly the many
humorous allusions, point to the earlier period; while the
large proportion of nature-myths, and the constant mention
of the greater divinities, could better be explained on the

---

[1] This is the opinion of the late R. A. Small, who in a dissertation
on *The Stage Quarrel between Ben Jonson and the So-called Poetasters,* Breslau, 1899, has made a study of the whole question *de novo,*
and has given an excellent summary of the preceding views.

hypothesis of the later date. If one had only these incidental allusions, the problem would be very baffling; but, fortunately, one has the play as a whole, a detailed, elaborate mythological allusion in five acts. To what period can we best assign this vast allusion to the myth of Troy? If Shakespeare had set himself to treat this subject at the time when he wrote the *Merchant of Venice,* he would have clothed it in the rich garment of poetry and romance. Recall for a moment those lines of Lorenzo quoted before, where Troilus mounts the Troyan walls and sighs for Cressid. They are hardly in the spirit of the drama which shows forth this same Troilus and Cressid. What, then, of Rosalind's playful words in *As You Like It?* They have been once quoted.

> Troilus had his brains dashed out with a Grecian club; yet he did what he could to die before, and he is one of the patterns of love.

That is more nearly in the tone of the drama, yet different enough. But suppose the disparaging, bantering spirit in which Shakespeare treats his mythology in *As You Like It* and *Much Ado* carried a little further. Would it not lead in all naturalness to the cynical, pitiless scorn with which, in *Troilus and Cressida,* he tears down the topless towers of his sorry Ilium? What are his Achilles and Patroclus but a *reductio ad absurdum* of classical heroism? The play should come, then, at the culmination of the period in which Shakespeare turned mythology to a jest; and consequently I should wish to assign it to a date some year or more later than *As You Like It,* in other words to 1601 or 1602, which is the exact date to which Dr. Small would assign it on wholly different grounds.[1] As further confirmation of this date, I would adduce the fact that all the allusions to the Troilus-story in the other dramas come before 1602, and that six of the seven fall between 1599 and 1602.[2] I should explain the large number of allusions to the greater divinities as an anticipation of the later treatment, showing itself at

---

[1] *Op. cit.*   [2] Cf. s. v. Troilus.

the very moment when the old was in its death-throes. Or it is just possible that the play may have received some revision at a later date. A similar attempt to determine the date of *Timon of Athens* will be found in Part Second.

IV

Turning now from matters of chronology and sources, it will be interesting to see in what ways Shakespeare incorporates the mythology of the ancients into the texture of his poetry. Though his acquaintance with the matter, drawn as it was from two or three Latin authors, was so limited as to blind him to many of the sublimer aspects of mythology, and though at times he seems to have accorded it but slight respect, it would be inconceivable that he should have failed to find in it much that his genius could turn to noble use.

Most obvious, perhaps, is his use of myth and fable to heighten the beauty of his verse by effective simile and metaphor. Thus Lucrece, in the first agonies of her disgrace, finds a sad comfort in comparing her unhappiness to that of the treacherously entreated Philomel,[1] and in scanning the scenes of woe depicted on the cloth of her chamber-wall, lingers over the story of perjured Sinon:

> For even as subtle Sinon here is painted,
> So sober-sad, so weary, and so mild,
> As if with grief or travail he had fainted,
> To me came Tarquin armed; so beguiled
> With outward honesty, but yet defiled
> With inward vice: as Priam him did cherish,
> So did I Tarquin; so my Troy did perish.[2]

It is in a similar spirit that the unhappy Richard contemplates his own failure:

> Down down I come; like glistering Phaeton,
> Wanting the manage of unruly jades.[3]

With less despondency, but with lively sense of peril, Portia

---

[1] Lucr. 1128 ff.   [2] Lucr. 1541-47.   [3] R2. 3. 3. 178-9.

waits while Bassanio makes his fateful choice. Her words
show that subtle blending of earnest seriousness and playful
humor, which is so characteristic of Shakespeare's women:

> Now he goes,
> With no less presence, but with much more love,
> Than young Alcides, when he did redeem
> The virgin tribute paid by howling Troy
> To the sea-monster: I stand for sacrifice;
> The rest aloof are the Dardanian wives,
> With bleared visages, come forth to view
> The issue of the exploit. Go, Hercules!
> Live thou, I live: with much much more dismay
> I view the fight than thou that makest the fray.[1]

Remembering a passage in Vergil, Hamlet is able to express
all the regal dignity of his murdered father in the lines:

> A station like the herald Mercury
> New-lighted on a heaven-kissing hill.[2]

How exquisitely Perdita suggests her own story by a mention of the lost Proserpina:

> O Proserpina,
> For the flowers now, that frighted thou let'st fall
> From Dis's waggon! daffodils,
> That come before the swallow dares, and take
> The winds of March with beauty; violets dim,
> But sweeter than the lids of Juno's eyes
> Or Cytherea's breath; pale primroses,
> That die unmarried, ere they can behold
> Bright Phœbus in his strength.[3]

Again, the whole story of the plain, blunt Ajax, cozened by
the wily, unscrupulous Ulysses, rises in the mind of Kent
when he sees himself worsted in words by the despicable
Oswald:

> None of these rogues and cowards
> But Ajax is their fool.[4]

Frequently the comparison is made in still subtler fashion

[1] Merch. 3. 2. 53-62. [2] Hml. 3. 4. 58-9.
[3] Wint. 4. 4. 116-124. [4] Lr. 2. 2. 131-2.

without explicit mention of the myth referred to.   It would strike us as incongruous were the serving-man, Adam, to refer more definitely to the poisoned shirt of Nessus; but we are aware of no incongruity when, impressed by the fact that it is the virtues of Orlando which inflame his brother against him, he exclaims:

> O, what a world is this, when what is comely
> Envenoms him that bears it![1]

Of a similar character is Duke Orsino's veiled allusion to the hounds of Actæon:

> O, when mine eyes did see Olivia first,
> Methought she purged the air of pestilence!
> That instant was I turn'd into a hart;
> And my desires, like fell and cruel hounds,
> E'er since pursue me.[2]

With unspeakable pathos, King Lear awakes from his long slumber, and imagining that he is dead and in hell, compares himself to Ixion on the wheel:

> You do me wrong to take me out o' the grave:
> Thou art a soul in bliss; but I am bound
> Upon a wheel of fire, that mine own tears
> Do scald like molten lead.[3]

I am inclined to think, however, that the aspect of mythology which appealed most deeply to Shakespeare, which he most fully and vitally incorporated into his own thoughts, is that original aspect of the system which gives a divine personality to the great forces of nature.   The sun in its rising and its setting, the 'gray-eyed dawn' and the 'black-browed night'; the procession of the seasons from 'well-apparelled April' to 'old Hiems' with his 'thin and icy crown'; 'Great Neptune's ocean' and the 'mutinous winds'; the crash of Jove's dread thunderbolt—to express his appreciation of all these, Shakespeare has constant recourse to the

---

[1] As 2. 3. 14-15.   [2] Tw. 1. 1. 19-23.   [3] Lr. 4. 7. 45-48.

forms of expression given us by the ancients, or, still more significantly, imitates their methods of thought without employing their exact terms. How thoroughly in accord with the spirit of mythology are Hotspur's words describing the fight between Mortimer and Glendower:

> Three times they breathed and three times did they drink,
> Upon agreement, of swift Severn's flood;
> Who then, affrighted with their bloody looks,
> Ran fearfully among the trembling reeds,
> And hid his crisp head in the hollow bank
> Bloodstained with these valiant combatants.[1]

Or again the simile in *King John* 3. 1. 23:

> Like a proud river peering o'er his bounds.

There is the germ of a whole myth in the lines:

> So looks the strand whereon the imperious flood
> Hath left a witness'd usurpation.[2]

Not only the war of the sea against the shore, but the ceaseless encounters of the sea and winds, 'old wranglers' (Troil. 2. 2. 75), takes on a personal aspect:

> Mad as the sea and wind, when both contend
> Which is the mightier.[3]

> And in the visitation of the winds,
> Who take the ruffian billows by the top,
> Curling their monstrous heads and hanging them
> With deafening clamor in the slippery clouds.[4]

Macbeth suggests[5] that the witches may 'untie the winds, and let them fight against the churches,' and in another passage[6] calls the winds 'sightless couriers of the air.'

Plato has told us that it is the work of the gods to bring order out of chaos; and so it is with the most godlike of men—philosophers, poets, artists; it must ever be their glory that they know how to transcend the conditions in which they

---

[1] H4A 1. 3. 102-107.   [2] H4B 1. 1. 62-3.   [3] Hml. 4. 1. 7-8.
[4] H4B 3. 1. 21-4.   [5] 4. 1. 52-3.   [6] 1. 7. 23.

live, to compel these conditions, hostile and discordant, into order and fair harmony, to impress the crude and stubborn material about them with the divine mark of the spiritual. It was so that Shakespeare compelled the conditions placed upon him by the dramatic traditions of his day; it was so, in a wider sense, that he took up into himself the rich and varied but discordant life of the Renaissance, and gave to it some of that order and spiritual harmony which is the glory of the greatest of mediæval art. It is this habit of thought and power of soul that seem to me evident in his treatment of the classical mythology. He did not know the great mythographers of Hellas, and was, in consequence, cut off from the sublimer aspects of their system; but from the mythology of Ovid and Vergil he was able to draw the poetic beauties which it offers, and while recognizing its limitations, to seek, not without success, for the deeper spiritual significance which it implies.

ABBREVIATIONS

___

THE PLAYS AND POEMS OF SHAKESPEARE.

Ado .....Much Ado About Nothing.
Alls .....All's Well That Ends Well.
Ant. .....Antony and Cleopatra.
As ....As You Like It.
Cæs. ....Julius Cæsar.
Cor. .....Coriolanus.
Cymb. ..Cymbeline.
Err. ......Comedy of Errors.
Gent. ....Two Gentlemen of Verona.
H4A ....Henry IV, Pt. I.
H4B ....Henry IV, Pt. II.
H5 ....Henry V.
H6A ....Henry VI, Pt. I.
H6B ....Henry VI, Pt. II.
H6C ....Henry VI, Pt. III.
H8 ....Henry VIII.
Hml. ....Hamlet.
K.J. .....King John.
LLL ....Love's Labor's Lost.
Lr. ....King Lear.
Lucr. ....Rape of Lucrece.

Mcb. .....Macbeth.
Meas. ....Measure for Measure.
Merch. ..Merchant of Venice.
Mids. ....Midsummer Night's Dream.
Oth. ......Othello.
Per. ......Pericles.
Pilgr. ....Passionate Pilgrim.
R2 ....Richard II.
R3 ....Richard III.
Rom. ....Romeo and Juliet.
Shr. ......Taming of the Shrew.
Sonn.....Sonnets.
Tim. .....Timon of Athens.
Tit. ....Titus Andronicus.
Tp. ......Tempest.
Troil. ....Troilus and Cressida.
Tw. ......Twelfth Night.
Ven. .....Venus and Adonis.
Wint. ....Winter's Tale.
Wiv. .....Merry Wives of Windsor.

Dir. ...Stage Direction.   Ind. ...Induction.   Prol. ...Prologue.

(These abbreviations are, with slight variations, those used by Schmidt in his Shakespeare Lexicon.)

VERGIL AND OVID.

Æn. .....Vergil's Æneis.
Am. ......Ovid's Amores.
Art. .,....Ovid's Ars Amatoria.
Fasti. ....Ovid's Fasti.
Georg. ...Vergil's Georgica.

Her. ....Ovid's Heroides.
Met. ....Ovid's Metamorphoses.
Pont. ...Ovid's Ex Ponto Epistulæ.
Trist. ...Ovid's Tristia.

PART FIRST

CLASSICAL MYTHOLOGY IN SHAKESPEARE

Absyrtus.—H6B 5. 2. 59. See Argonauts.

Acheron.—See Hades.

Achilles.—LLL 5. 2. 635; Lucr. 1424; H6B 5. 1. 100; Troil. passim.

Outside of Troil. Achilles is mentioned only three times. In LLL he is the antagonist of Hector. In Lucr. he is one of the figures in the painting of Troy, and his spear is mentioned. In H6B the spear is mentioned in more detail:

> That gold must round engirt these brows of mine,
> Whose smile and frown, like to Achilles' spear,
> Is able with the change to kill and cure.

King Telephus was wounded by Achilles' spear and learned from the oracle that he could only be cured by him who had inflicted the wound. This Achilles accomplished by some of the rust from his spear. The primary authority for this story is Dictys Cretensis 2. 10; but it is alluded to several times by Ovid: *Met.* 12. 112; *Trist.* 5. 2. 15; *Pont.* 2. 2. 26. In *Met.* 13. 171-72 we read 'Ego Telephon hasta Pugnantem domui, victum orantemque refeci.' This Golding renders (p. 162b):

> I did wound
> King Teleph with his speare, and when he lay uppon the ground,
> I was intreated with the speare too heale him safe and sound.

In Troil. he is a brave and mighty warrior, but excessively proud. Agamemnon says that he is 'in self-assumption greater than in the note of judgment,' 2. 3. 133. He is called 'broad Achilles' in 1. 3. 190. Caxton says of him, p. 541, 'Achilles was of right grete beaulte/ blonke heeris & cryspe graye eyen and grete/ of Amyable sighte/ large brestes & brode sholdres grete Armes/ his raynes hyghe

ynowh/ an hyghe man of grete stature/ and had no pareyll
ne like to hym amonge alle the grekes/ desiryng to fighte/
large in yeftes and outerageous in dispense.' His pride
could have been learned from Chapman's Homer. From
the same source would come the fact several times mentioned
in the play that he is son of Thetis. The phrase 'great
Thetis' son,' 3. 3. 94, is to be found verbatim in Chapman *Il.*
7 (p. 98). The main features of his action in Troil. are
taken from Caxton.

The Myrmidons are mentioned in the nonsense of the
clown, Feste, in Tw. 2. 3. 29. The name occurs in Caxton
and Homer.

Actæon.—Wiv. 2. 1. 122; 3. 2. 44; Tw. 1. 1. 22; Tit. 2. 3. 63, 70-71.

The story of Actæon is told at length in *Met.* 3. 138-252.
That Shakespeare had read this passage in Golding's translation is proved by Pistol's comparing Master Ford to 'Sir
Actæon, with Ringwood at his heels' (Wiv. 2. 1. 122).
Ovid gives the names of all Actæon's hounds. The last in
the list is Hylactor (l. 224). Golding substitutes English
dog-names throughout, and 'Hylactor' is represented by
'Ringwood.' As the last in a long list, it would have the
best chance of sticking in the reader's memory.

In the first two and the last of the passages cited above,
the myth becomes a variation of the ever-recurring horn
joke.

A more pleasing adaptation is that of Tw. 1. 1. 22, where
Duke Orsino says:

> O, when mine eyes did see Olivia first,
> Methought she purged the air of pestilence.
> That instant was I turn'd into a hart;
> And my desires, like fell and cruel hounds,
> E'er since pursue me.

The conceit may have been borrowed from the fifth sonnet
of Daniel's *Delia* (1592).

Adonis.—Ven.; Pass. Pilg. 4; 6; 9; Shr. Ind. 2. 52; Sonn. 53. 5; H6A 1. 6. 6.

The sources of Shakespeare's *Venus and Adonis* have been well demonstrated by Thomas Baynes in an article called *What Shakespeare learned at School, Fraser's Mag.* (New Series) 21. 629-632. After carefully examining the ground, I am able to add only one or two additional proofs of the correctness of his conclusions.

Shakespeare's story combines two of Ovid's fables: that of Venus and Adonis, *Met.* 10. 519-559, 705-739, and that of Salmacis and Hermaphrodite, *Met.* 4. 285-388. In the first of these fables only the outline of the story is given. Venus, accidentally wounded by Cupid's arrow, falls in love with the boy Adonis, and, in her pursuit of him, adopts the garb of Diana and hunts the less dangerous beasts. She counsels Adonis to avoid boars, wolves, bears, and lions. She especially detests the boar. Adonis asks why. They recline side by side under the shade of a poplar, while she tells him the story of Atalanta (ll. 560-704). After the warning she departs. Adonis hunts the boar and is killed. Venus, returning, mourns over him, and has him metamorphosed into the anemone. Of the bashfulness and persistent coldness of Adonis there is no hint. For this the story of Salmacis is unquestionably the source.

That Shakespeare had before him the passage in *Met.* 10 is proved by the following cases of imitation:

> Sic ait, ac mediis interserit oscula verbis.
> *Met.* 10. 559.

with which cf. Ven. 47, 54, 59.

> Non movet ætas
> Nec facies nec quæ Venerem movere, leones
> Sætigerosque sues, oculosque animosque ferarum.
> *Met.* 10. 547-549.

with which cf. Ven. 631-632.

> Tutæque animalia prædæ,
> Aut pronos lepores, aut celsum in cornua cervum,
> Aut agitat dammas.
> *Met.* 10. 537-539.

with which cf. Ven. 674-676, though the application is changed, as also in the following quotation which is to be compared with Ven. 884-885 :

> A fortibus abstinet apris,
> Raptoresque lupos armatosque unguibus ursos
> Vitat et armenti saturatos cæde leones.
>
> *Met.* 10. 539-541.

A cursory reading of Ovid's fable of Salmacis will convince one that Shakespeare has combined that story with the fable of Venus and Adonis. Further proof of this confusion is furnished by an examination of sonnets 4 and 6 of the Passionate Pilgrim, which are accepted as Shakespeare's. In each, Cytherea is 'sitting by a brook'—a scene which corresponds with the setting of the Salmacis story better than with that of Ovid's Venus and Adonis. In l. 5 of sonnet 4,

> She told him stories to delight his ear,

we have a return to the story of Venus and Adonis (see above), but the rest of the sonnet takes us back to Salmacis. The whole situation of sonnet 6 is obviously imitated from Ovid's Salmacis, and ll. 10-11,

> The sun look'd on the world with glorious eye,
> Yet not so wistly as this queen on him,

strongly suggest *Met.* 4. 347-49 :

> Flagrant quoque lumina nymphæ
> Non aliter quam cum puro nitidissimus orbe
> Opposita speculi referitur imagine Phœbus.

Sonnet 9 of the Passionate Pilgrim deals also with Venus and Adonis, but the incident is probably of Shakespeare's invention.

Baynes has noticed that the description of the boar in Ven. 619-621 is imitated from that of the Calydonian boar in *Met.* 8. 284-86 :

> On his bow-back he hath a battle set
> Of bristly pikes, that ever threat his foes;
> His eyes like glow-worms shine when he doth fret.

Sanguine et igne micant oculi, riget ardua cervix,
Et setæ similes rigidis hastilibus horrent
Stantque velut vallum, velut alta hastilia setæ.

Whether Shakespeare read these passages of Ovid in the original or in Golding's translation, it is impossible to say with any certainty. In two instances only is there any verbal similarity between Shakespeare and Golding. At the end of sonnet 4 of the Pass. Pilg. we read:

He rose and ran away; ah, fool too froward!

On page 57a of Golding, Salmacis calls Hermaphrodite 'froward boy.' The description of the boar is given by Golding in these words:

His eies did glister blud and fire: right dreadfull was to see
His brawned necke, right dredfull was his heare which grew as thicke
With pricking points as one of them could well by other sticke.
And like a front of armed *Pikes set* close in *battall* ray,
The sturdie *bristles* on his back stoode staring up alway.
(p. 107a)

In H6A we read:

Thy promises are like Adonis' gardens
That one day bloom'd and fruitful were the next.

The gardens are mentioned by Pliny, *N. H.* 19. 19. 1; but in all probability the author is indebted to the long description of them in Spenser, *F. Q.* 3. 6. Stanza 42 says that continual spring and harvest meet together there, and both blossoms and fruit are found side by side.

Ægle.—Mids. 2. 1. 79. See Theseus.

Æneas.—Mids. 1. 1. 174; Hml. 2. 2. 468; Cæs. 1. 2. 112; Ant. 4. 14. 53; Tp. 2. 1. 79; Cymb. 3. 4. 60; Troil. passim. Tit. 3. 2. 27; 5. 3. 80; H6B 3. 2. 118.

The slightly developed character of Æneas in Troil. is probably drawn from Caxton's summary of his character on p. 543 of the *Recuyell*: 'Eneas had a grete body discrete mervayllously in his werkis well bespoken and attempryd in his wordes. Full of good counceyll and of science connyng

3

He had his visage Ioyouse/ and the eyen clere and graye.'
In the plays he is mentioned seldom.   Twice he is referred
to as bearing Anchises on his shoulders, Cæs. 1. 2. 112,
H6B 5. 2. 62 (cf. *Æn.* 2. 707).   In every other instance he
is mentioned in connection with Dido (*q. v.*).   In Cymb.
he is 'false Æneas,' where, though Dido is not mentioned,
the connection is obvious.   Twice (Cæs. 1. 2. 112; Tit. 3. 2.
27) he is ancestor of the Romans.   That Venus is his
mother would be gathered from his oath by Anchises and
Venus in Troil. 4. 1. 21.   Of his adventures after leaving
Dido, there is no hint in Shakespeare.

Æolus.—H6B 3. 2. 92; Per. 3. 1. 2.

In H6B Æolus is spoken of as loosing the winds from
their 'brazen caves,' and in Per. he is implored to 'bind
them in brass.'   This is to be referred to *Od.* 10. 2, where
the island of Æolus is said to have a τεῖχος χάλκεον.   There is
no mention of brass in the Vergilian account.

Æsculapius.—Per. 3. 2. 111.

'Æsculapius guide us,' i. e. in a case of medical treatment.
Æsculapius is the god of the medical art, or as in Homer, a
'blameless physician' (*Il.* 4. 194).   In *Met.* 15. 535 the dis-
membered body of Hippolytus is restored 'by Æsculapius
meanes', as Golding renders the 'ope Pæonia' of the original.
In *Met.* 15. 622 ff. Ovid describes how Æsculapius was
brought to Rome.   Again Golding supplies his name (p.
196b), which is suppressed in the Latin.

Æson.—Merch. 5. 1. 13.   See Argonauts.

Agamemnon.—H4B 2. 4. 237; H5. 3. 6. 7; H6C 2. 2. 148; Troil.
passim.

The Agamemnon of Troil. is not deeply characterized.
He is the chief commander, and his opening speech is not
without kingliness, but he is by no means the most prominent Greek on the stage.   The character may have been
drawn from Caxton, from Homer, or from mere tradition.

He is mentioned three times in the other dramas. In H4B he is a type of valor; in H5 the Welshman, Fluellen, says that the Duke of Exeter is 'as magnanimous as Agememnon.' The epithet *magnanimus* is used by Ovid and Vergil of several of the heroes, but never of Agamemnon. It translates μεγάθυμος of Homer; but in Homer this epithet is not peculiar to Agamemnon. He is mentioned as brother of Menelaus in H6C.

Agenor.—Ado 5. 4. 45. The father of Europa. See Jupiter.

Ajax.—LLL 4. 3. 7; 5. 2. 581; Lucr. 1394, 1398; Lr. 2. 2. 133; Ant. 4. 13. 2; 4. 14. 38; Cymb. 4. 2. 252; H6B 5. 1. 26; Tit. 1. 1. 379; Shr. 3. 1. 53; and Troil. passim.

Shakespeare's knowledge of Ajax is to a great extent drawn from the account of his dispute with Ulysses over the armor of Achilles given by Ovid in *Met.* 13. Ulysses, by his cunning speech, persuades the Greeks to award the armor to him, on which Ajax, overcome by grief and chagrin, goes mad and kills himself with his own sword. To this dispute Shakespeare refers in several passages. Thus we find the two heroes mentioned together in the description of the Troy picture in Lucr., the blunt rage of Ajax contrasting with the mild, sly glance of Ulysses. So, too, in Lr. when Kent is rebuked by Cornwall for the bluntness of his speech, he exclaims: 'None of these rogues and cowards but Ajax is their fool.' This I should paraphrase as follows: 'I am a plain blunt fellow like Ovid's Ajax. You, Oswald, are a smooth talker like Ulysses. (Ajax calls him rogue and coward in Ovid.) The Ulysses is always able to make a fool of the Ajax and get the better of him as you do now of me.' From the same passage in *Met.* Shakespeare might have learned of the 'seven-fold shield' of Ajax, referred to in Ant. 4. 14. 38, the 'clipeus septemplex' of *Met.* 13. 2; so too the fact mentioned in Shr. that Ajax was called Æacides from his grandfather. Still another allusion to the dispute is found in Ant. 4. 13. 2.

In his drama, *Ajax,* Sophocles describes further how in his madness Ajax slaughtered sheep and oxen, and how after his death, his rival, Ulysses, persuaded the Greeks to grant him honorable burial. To the slaughter of the cattle we find allusion in LLL 4 and H6B, and in Tit. to the intercession of Ulysses. We must not, however, assume too hastily that Shakespeare was acquainted with Sophocles, for the story of the cattle is mentioned in Horace, *Sat.* 2. 3. 202, and Ritson says that it is embodied in one of the proverbs of Fuller's *Gnomologia;* for the intercession of Ulysses it is not so easy to find a source outside of Sophocles.

The character of Ajax as shown in Troil. requires special comment. From the testimony of the other characters, and from the actions of Ajax himself, we find him a vain braggart, self-willed, stupid. This is not the Ajax of Homer nor of Caxton, who furnish the main incidents of his action. So great is the disparity that R. A. Small in *The Stage-Quarrel between Ben Jonson and the So-called Poetasters,* Breslau, 1899, thinks Shakespeare has invented the characterization as a satire on Jonson. But the Ajax of Troil. is the Ajax of Ulysses's speech in *Met.* 13. He is called in Golding's translation 'dolt and grossehead' (p. 162a), 'hath neyther wit nor knowledge' (p. 164b), etc. His vaunting is mentioned on p. 163b and his whole speech claiming the arms justifies the charge.

He is called Ajax Telamonius in H6B, and in Ant. 4. 13 merely Telamon.

Alcides.—See Hercules.

Alecto.—Ant. 2. 5. 40. See Furies.

Althæa.—H4B 2. 2. 93, 96; H6B 1. 1. 234.

In H4B the Page calls the red-faced Bardolph 'rascally Althæa's dream,' and explains: 'Althæa dreamed she was delivered of a firebrand; and therefore I call him her dream.' On this Dr. Johnson comments: 'Shakespeare is here mistaken in his mythology, and has confounded Althæa's firebrand with Hecuba's. The firebrand of Althæa was real; but Hecuba, when she was big with Paris, dreamed that she was delivered of a firebrand which consumed the kingdom.' Hecuba's dream is described in Ovid, *Her.* 16. 45-46.

The true Althæa's brand is alluded to in H6B, which is to be referred to *Met.* 8. 260-547. Paris is rightly called a 'firebrand' in Troil. 2. 2. 110. (See Paris.)

Amazons.—K. J. 5. 2. 155; Cor. 2. 2. 95; Tim. 1. 2. 136; H6A
1. 2. 104; H6C 1. 4. 114; 4. 1. 106.

The term is used of women who, as La Pucelle for example, take part in war. It is impossible to assign any source for so common an idea.

Amphion (?)

In Tp. 2. 1. 87 Sebastian says: 'His word is more than the miraculous harp; he hath raised the wall and houses too.' That Amphion raised the walls of Thebes with his music, is mentioned in *Met.* 6. 178. Golding translates (p. 77b):

This same towne whose walles my husbands harpe did frame.

W. A. Wright says that it may rather be Apollo who raised the walls of Troy. The miraculous harp of Apollo is mentioned in *Her.* 16. 180.

Anchises.—Cæs. 1. 2. 114; Troil. 4. 1. 21; H6B 5. 2. 62. See Æneas.

Anna.—Shr. 1. 1. 159. See Dido.

Antiopa.—Mids. 2. 1. 80. See Theseus.

Apollo.

Except in a single epithet 'fire-robed' (Wint. 4. 4. 30), there is no suggestion that Shakespeare connects Apollo with the sun, which he personifies so often under the name of Phœbus. (See Sun-divinities.) It is as patron of music and of learning that Shakespeare regards him. As motto to one of his earliest works, the Ven., he quoted two lines from Ovid (*Am.* 1. 15. 35-36) which show Apollo in this capacity:

Vilia miretur vulgus; mihi flavus Apollo
Pocula Castalia plena ministret aqua.

In LLL we find the simile: 'As sweet and musical as bright Apollo's lute, strung with his hair'—a conceit which is probably Shakespeare's own, though the beauty of Apollo's hair is implied in the epithet 'flavus.' Apollo is also patron of music in LLL 5. 2. 941; Troil. 3. 3. 305; Shr. Ind. 2. 37. He is patron of learning in Per. 3. 2. 67 and probably also in Troil. 1. 3. 328. In Troil. 2. 2. 79 he is merely a type of beauty.

In Wint. Leontes consults the oracle at Delphi as to his wife's chastity, and in consequence Apollo's name occurs frequently, especially in Acts 2 and 3. It is to be noticed that Shakespeare considers Delphi an island (3. 1. 2), a mistake which he borrows from *Dorastus and Fawnia* (Hazlitt's *Shak. Libr.* Pt. 1. Vol. 4. p. 39), from which he takes the whole incident of consulting the oracle. The 'ysle of Delphi' is also mentioned by Caxton, p. 548 etc.

Lear's oath by Apollo (Lr. 1. 1. 162) may be explained by the fact that Holinshed says that a 'temple of Apollo stood in the citie of Troinouant' (London) (Boswell-Stone's *Shakespeare's Holinshed,* p. 5, note).

Of the mythology in a narrower sense, there is a mere allusion to Apollo's metamorphosis into a shepherd for the deception of Isse (*Met.* 6. 122) taken over bodily from *Dorastus and Fawnia* (Hazlitt's *Shak. Libr.* Pt. I. Vol. 4. p. 62.) in Wint. 4. 4. 30; and three allusions to the fable of Apollo and Daphne: Mids. 2. 1. 231; Troil. 1. 1. 101; Shr. Ind. 2. 61. Shakespeare may well have learned the story from *Met.* 1. 452 seq. More explicit is the reference in Shr. where the servant, having offered various pictures to poor Sly, suggests:

> Or Daphne roaming through a thorny wood,
> Scratching her legs that one shall swear she bleeds,
> And at that sight shall sad Apollo weep.

With this cf. *Met.* 1. 508-9; Apollo says:

> Alas alas how woulde it greeve my hart,
> Too see thee fall among the briers, and that the blud shoulde start
> Out of thy tender legges, I wretch the causer of thy smart.
> (Golding, p. 11b)

Aquilon.—Troil. 4. 5. 9.

The north wind. Only twice does Shakespeare personify the winds under classical names: here and in Troil. 1. 3. 38 where Boreas is mentioned, both times, it will be observed, in the same play. The particular expression:

> Blow, villain, till thy sphered bias cheek
> Outswell the colic of puff'd Aquilon

suggests the

> Blow winds, and crack your cheeks

of Lr. 3. 2. 1. In each case the allusion is to the conventional pictorial representation of the winds as cherubs with puffed cheeks. (Cf. Botticelli's Venus.)

The names Boreas and Aquilon occur in Vergil.

Arachne (Ariachne).—Troil. 5. 2. 152.

Arachne is the maiden, who, presuming to vie with Minerva in weaving, was for her arrogance turned into a spider. *Met.* 6. 1-145.

By 'Ariachne's broken woof' Shakespeare means, apparently, cobweb. (Cf. K. J. 4. 3. 128.) The passage would then be paraphrased: 'No opening large enough for a thread of cobweb to enter.' The phrase 'broken woof,' however, is suggestive of the Ovidian story. Shakespeare's mistaken form of the name is to be traced to confusion with Ariadne, who is also famed for her thread.

Argonauts.—Merch. 1. 1. 170-172; 3. 2. 244; 5. 1. 13; H6B 5. 2. 59.

It is worthy of notice that all the allusions to the Argonauts in the genuine plays occur in Merch. The winning of the golden fleece is alluded to in the first two passages, for which the source is to be found in *Met.* 7. 1 seq. in Golding's translation, as shown by the phrase 'Colchos strand' (Merch. 1. 1. 171), evidently taken from the following line on p. 89b of Golding:

And so with conquest and a wife he loosde from Colchos strond.

(*Colchos i*s a frequent spelling in 16th century books.)
   In Merch, 5. 1. 13 we read:

> In such a night
> Medea gather'd the enchanted herbs
> That did renew old Æson.

The mention of Medea after Thisbe and Dido, whose stories are related consecutively in that order in the *Legend of Good Women,* would make us look to the *Legend* as a source, but we find there no mention of the 'renewal' of Æson.   The story is told at length in *Met.* 7. 159-293.   In l. 180 we learn that the magic herbs were gathered under a full moon, which is the point of allusion.   From this passage of *Met.* in Golding's translation Shakespeare later borrowed Prospero's incantation in Tp. 5. 1. 33 ff.   The presumption that Shakespeare read the passage in Golding is further strengthened by the lines on p. 92:

And as from dull unweeldsome age to youth he backwarde drew;
Even so a lively youthfull spright did in his hart *renew,*

which depart widely from the Latin original.

   The story of Medea and Absyrtus, alluded to in H6B 5. 2. 59, is told by Ovid in *Trist.* 3. 9.

Argus.—LLL 3. 1. 201; Merch. 5. 1. 230; Troil. 1. 2. 31.

   The monster with a hundred eyes set by the jealous Juno to guard Io.   He is lulled asleep by the music of Mercury, *Met.* 1. 621 seq.   By a strange confusion with the Hydra, the charming asleep of Argus' eyes is mentioned in connection with Hydra in H4B 4. 2. 38.   (Cf. s. v. Hercules.)

Ariadne.—Gent. 4. 4. 172; Mids. 2. 1. 80.

   In Gent. we read:

> Madam, 'twas Ariadne passioning
> For Theseus' perjury and unjust flight.

Shakespeare may have in mind *Her.* 10, which is one long 'passioning' of Ariadne, (or Chaucer's imitation of it, *Legend of Good Women* 2185 ff.) which he imitates in

Merch. (see Dido). The word 'perjury' suggests *Fasti* 3. 469 seq.:

> Flebat amans coniunx, spatiataque litore curvo
> Edidit incultis talia verba comis:
> 'En iterum, fluctus, similis audite querellas!
> En iterum lacrimas accipe, harena, meas!
> Dicebam, memini, "periure et perfide Theseu!"'

He is called *periurus* also in *Am.* 1. 7. 15. Ariadne is mentioned as a forsaken love of Theseus in Mids., where the name may have been taken from North's Plutarch, *Theseus,* p. 73 (see Theseus).

Arion.—Tw. 1. 2. 15.

The story of Arion is told by Ovid, *Fasti* 2. 83 seq.; but the story was, of course, common property. Cf. Spenser, *F. Q.* 4. 11. 23. It is noticeable that Shakespeare does not refer to him as a musician.

Ascanius.—H6B 3. 2. 116.

Mentioned as Æneas' son, relating his father's acts to Dido. See Dido.

Astræa.—Tit. 4. 3. 4; H6A 1. 6. 4.

In Tit. the words 'Terras Astræa reliquit' are quoted exactly from *Met.* 1. 150, and the idea is further expanded at ll. 39. 49 of the same scene. In H6A Charles calls La Pucelle: 'Divinest creature, Astræa's daughter,' meaning possibly that in rescuing Orleans she has made justice prevail, or perhaps associating her with the Golden Age, before Astræa left the earth.

Atalanta.—As. 3. 2. 155; 3. 2. 293.

In the second passage there is a reference to Atalanta's heels: that is her swiftness. The story is told in *Met.* 10. 560-704. What is meant by 'Atalanta's better part' in the first passage has caused long discussion (see Furness' Var.).

That Dr. Furness is right in deciding it to be her beauty is
supported by the antithesis implied in ll. 562-3:

> And hard it is to tell
> Thee whither she did in footemanshippe or beawty more excell.
> (Golding, p. 137a)

Ate.—LLL 5. 2. 694; K. J. 2. 1. 63; Ado 2. 1. 263; Cæs. 3. 1. 271.

In the first passage Biron says: 'More Ates! more Ates!
stir them on! stir them on!' In K. J. and Cæs. there is the
same idea of stirring on to blood and strife. In Ado Benedick says of Beatrice: 'You shall find her the infernal Ate
in good apparel.' Ate is the spirit of discord inciting to
war. She is referred to at some length in *Iliad* 19. 91 seq.
but Chapman's translation did not appear till 1611. In
Latin literature the name does not occur at all. Where
then did Shakespeare learn it? Furness suggests Spenser,
Faerie Queene 4. 1. 19-30, where she is described in detail,
but unfortunately there is a discrepancy of dates. Book IV
of the *F. Q.* was not published till 1598, while K. J. is
assigned to 1595 and LLL cannot be later than 1591 (though
perhaps revised in 1598). Ate is also mentioned in *F. Q.*
2. 7. 55 (pub. 1590) as having thrown the apple of discord,
but the allusion is only a passing one. Perhaps Shakespeare
learned her name from Peele's *Arraignment of Paris* (1584)
in which she appears as Prologue, calling herself 'condemned
soul, Ate, from lowest hell.' She is identical with the Dis-
cordia of *Æn.* 6. 280, who is one of the dwellers in hell-
mouth. The 'Ate in good apparel' of Ado may be in contrast to the line:

> Et *scissa* gaudens vadit Discordia *palla*

of *Æn.* 8. 702. Cf. also Statius, *Theb.* 1. 109, where the
poet is describing Tisiphone.

Atlas.—Ant. 1. 5. 23; H6C 5. 1. 36.

Cleopatra calls Antony the 'demi-Atlas of this earth.' In
Met. 4. 662 Atlas is mentioned as supporting the heavens on
his shoulders. The idea is a commonplace.

Aurora.

Aurora is mentioned by name only twice: Mids. 3. 2. 380; Rom. 1. 1. 142. In the first instance she is merely the dawn, and the morning star is called her harbinger. In the second passage there is more significance:

> But all so soon as the all-cheering sun
> Should in the furthest east begin to draw
> The shady curtains from Aurora's bed.

This would apparently mean that the sun drew the curtains *and left* her bed. Such an interpretation is supported by several passages in which 'morning' is personified. Thus in Ven. 855:

> And wakes the morning, from whose silver breast
> The sun ariseth in his majesty.

and in H6C 2. 1. 21:

> See how the morning opes her golden gates,
> And takes her farewell of the glorious sun.

Cf. also Ven. 1; Tit. 2. 1. 5. The passage in H6C evidently regards the sun as a lover sent forth by Morning to run his course and return to her again. If this interpretation is correct, it will furnish an explanation to a disputed passage in Mids. (3. 2. 389): Puck says:

> My fairy lord, this must be done with haste,
> For night's swift dragons cut the clouds full fast,
> And yonder shines Aurora's harbinger;

at whose approach all spirits must vanish. To this Oberon replies:

> But we are spirits of another sort:
> I with the *morning's love* have oft made sport.

Who is the 'morning's love' with whom Oberon has sported? Shakespeare never mentions Tithonus; it seems to me improbable that Cephalus is intended. May it not be the sun? Oberon would then be made to say, 'I have often sported in sunlight'—an answer which meets Puck's objection. That this conception is not peculiar to Shakespeare may be shown by Chaucer, *Troilus and Criseyde* 3. 1464-7:

> And eek the sonne Tytan gan he chyde,
> And seyde, 'O fool, wel may men thee dispyse,
> That hast the Dawing al night by thy syde,
> And suffrest hir so sone up fro thee ryse.'

One is tempted to ask whether there may not have been some confusion of the names *Titan* and *Tithonus*.

Autolycus.—Wint. 4. 3. 24, etc.

The Autolycus of Ovid is a son of Mercury, 'furtum ingeniosus ad omne . . . . patriæ non degener artis' *Met.* 11. 313-315. In Wint. he is 'littered under Mercury,' and is 'a snapper up of unconsidered trifles.'

Bacchus.—LLL 4. 3. 339; Ant. 2. 7. 121.

In the first passage 'dainty Bacchus' is spoken of as having a delicate taste; in the second, he is addressed in a drinking song as 'monarch of the vine, Plumpy Bacchus with pink eyne.' This conception is thoroughly conventional, and cannot be assigned to a particular source.

Bellona.—Mcb. 1. 2. 54.

Macbeth is called 'Bellona's bridegroom.' As Clarendon has suggested, this may be a reminiscence of 'et Bellona manet te pronuba' of *Æn.* 7. 319. Cf. Massinger, *Bondman* 1. 1. 13-14:

> I'd court Bellona in her horrid trim
> As if she were a mistress.

Boreas.—Troil. 1. 3. 38. See Aquilon.

Briareus.—Troil. 1. 2. 30.

Merely alluded to as having 'many hands.' Vergil mentions 'centumgeminus Briareus' in the descent into Hades. *Æn.* 6. 287. Cf. also Hom. *Il.* 1. 403.

Calydonian Boar.—Ant. 4. 13. 2.

'The boar of Thessaly was never so embossed.' Calydon
is in Ætolia instead of Thessaly, but the two provinces are
not far apart. Embossed means 'foaming at the mouth'
(Schmidt). In *Met.* 8. 288, 417, this detail is mentioned.
The first of these passages is that copied by Shakespeare in
Ven. (cf. s. v. Adonis).

Centaurs.—Mids. 5. 1. 44; Hml. 4. 7. 88; Lr. 4. 6. 126; Troil.
    5. 5. 14; Tit. 5. 2. 204.

In Lr. Shakespeare uses the Centaur, half human, half
horse, as a type of the bestiality of human nature:

> Down from the waist they are Centaurs,
> Though women all above.

The idea is one that might easily occur to Shakespeare independently of any source. Still, in Ovid the Centaurs are
given to lust and violence, as Nessus who attempted the
rape of Deianira (see Hercules) and the Centaurs at the
marriage feast of Hippodamia. At this, one of the Centaurs
tries to violate the bride; and the feast ends in a bloody
battle between the Centaurs and Lapithæ. *Met.* 12. 210 seq.
This feast is twice alluded to in Shakespeare: Mids. 5. 1. 44;
Tit. 5. 2. 204. Especially appropriate is the allusion in Tit.,
for Ovid's story is told with a wealth of revolting detail
rivalling that of Tit. In Mids. Theseus reads:

> 'The battle with the Centaurs, to be sung
> By an Athenian eunuch to the harp.'
> We'll none of that: that have I told my love
> In glory of my kinsman Hercules.

Hercules' battle with the Centaurs was not the same as the
battle of Centaurs and Lapithæ (cf. Apollod. 2. 5. 4 and
Diod. 4. 33), but the two battles were very early confused.
In *Met.* 12, when Nestor has finished the account of the battle over Hippodamia, Tlepolemus says (ll. 539-541):

> Herculeæ mirum est oblivia laudis
> Acti tibi, senior. Certe mihi sæpe referre
> Nubigenas domitos a se pater ipse solebat.

The same confusion is to be noticed in North's Plutarch, *Theseus,* p. 75, in Caxton, p. 315 ff., and in Spenser, *F. Q.* 4. 1. 23.   In Hml. 4. 7. 88 a good horseman is compared to a Centaur, *tacito nomine.*   (Cf. Jonson, *Underwoods* 71.) The 'dreadful Sagittary' of Troil. 5. 5. 14 is a Centaur who, as Caxton tells us, came to the aid of the Trojans.   'The Centaur' is the name of an inn in Err.

Cephalus and Procris.—Mids. 5. 1. 201, 202.

> Not Shefalus to Procrus was so true.

The mechanicals have mispronounced the names of the Ovidian couple.   The fidelity of Cephalus is related in *Met.* 7. 690 seq.   A poem called *Procris and Cephalus* was entered on the Stat. Reg. on 22 Oct. 1593.   The poem is attributed to Anthony Chute, but there seems to be reason for thinking it not by Chute, but by Thomas Edwards (*Dict. Nat. Biog.* s. v. Chute).   The date of Mids. has been placed as early as 1590, and as late as 1595.

Cerberus.—LLL 5. 2. 593; H4B 2. 4. 182; Troil. 2. 1. 37; Tit. 2. 4. 51.

Cerberus disputes the passage of Æneas in *Æn.* 6. 417-425, but the sibyl stupefies him with a drugged cake.   Shakespeare mentions him in connection with Hercules (LLL) and with Orpheus (Tit.).   See under Hercules and Orpheus. The 'King Cerberus' of H4B is one of Pistol's confusions, and has nothing to do with the canine subject of this paragraph.   For the reference to Cerberus and Proserpina in Troil., I find no definite authority.

Ceres.—Tp. 4. 1. 60-138; H6B 1. 2. 2.

In the masque in Tp. Ceres appears as the divinity who presides over the 'foison plenty' of earth's increase.   The editors have pointed out the fact, that in making her preside over the 'pole-clipt vineyard' and the 'sea-marge, sterile and rocky-hard,' the author expands her strictly classical character as goddess of grain.   In the same passage she is recognized as mother of Proserpina (cf. *Met.* 5. 359-550). In H6B the phrase 'Ceres' plenteous load' is equivalent to 'weight of grain.'

Charon.—R3. 1. 4. 46; Troil. 3. 2. 11.   See Hades.

Charybdis.—Merch. 3. 5. 19.   See Scylla.

Cimmerian.—Tit. 2. 3. 72.

Aaron, the moor, is called a 'swart Cimmerian.'   The land of the Cimmerians at the gate of Hades is described in *Od.* 11. 14 seq.   'Never on them does the shining sun look down with his beams . . . . but deadly night is spread abroad over these hapless men.'   But the men are not described as of swart skin.   Does Shakespeare confuse them with the Ethiopians?   Johnson says: 'The Moor is called Cimmerian from the affinity of blackness to darkness.' The phrase 'darke Cimmerians' occurs in Golding, p. 147b, at the beginning of the description of the Cave of Sleep, where the original has no epithet.   (*Met.* 11. 592.)

Circe.—Err. 5. 1. 270; H6A 5. 3. 35.

In Err. the Duke says:

> Why what an intricate impeach is this!
> I think you all have drunk of Circe's cup.

On this Malone remarks: 'Circe's cup turned men to swine but did not deprive them of their reason.'   But the Duke merely means that there has been a change of form and consequent confusion.   Cf. also Err. 3. 2. 151.   In H6A:

> See how the ugly witch doth bend her brows,
> As if with Circe she would change my shape!

Homer's account of Circe in *Od.* 10. 133-260 is retold at length by Ovid in *Met.* 14. 244-309, where Shakespeare probably became acquainted with it.   Circe is also mentioned in *Æn.* 7. 10-20.   In Ovid's version Circe's *cup* (*pocula*) is twice mentioned.

Cocytus.—See Hades.

Cressida.—See Troilus.

Cupid.

Shakespeare's mentions of Cupid (or of Love as equivalent to Cupid) are very numerous. The epithets and attributes are those common to all his contemporaries. He is a boy, the son of Venus (As 4. 1. 216), in 21 passages armed with bow and arrow, 20 times referred to as blind, 7 times as winged, 3 times with a firebrand. Except for the quality of blindness all these attributes are to be found in Ovid. For the bow cf. *Am.* 2. 9. 5, etc.; for the wings, *Art.* 1. 233; for the brand, *Am.* 2. 9. 5. This late Roman tradition is very widespread. Isidore (died 636) explains these attributes in *Origines* 8. 11. 80; 'Qui ideo alatus pingitur quia nihil amantibus levius, nihil mutabilius invenitur: Puer pingitur quia stultus est et irrationabilis amor: Sagittam et facem tenere fingitur; sagittam quia amor cor vulnerat, facem quia inflammat.' A passage closely resembling this is to be found in *Mythographi* 2. fab. 33, ed. Mai, in *Classicorum Auctorum e Vaticanis Codicibus Editorum,* Tom. III., Romæ, 1831. Cf. also Propertius, *Eleg.* 2. 12. Closely resembling these passages in manner is Mids. 1. 1. 234 ff.:

> Love looks not with the eyes, but with the mind;
> And therefore is wing'd Cupid painted blind, etc.

For the blindness of Cupid I find no classical authority whatever; but the notion was already common in Chaucer (*Hous of Fame* 138, etc.) and Gower (*Conf. Am.* 3. 1465; 5. 1417; etc).

More specific is the allusion to the *golden* arrow in Ven. 947; Tw. 1. 1. 35, and in the following lines from Mids. 1. 1. 169-170:

> I swear to thee by Cupid's strongest bow,
> By his best arrow with the golden head.

This is to be traced ultimately to *Met.* 1. 466. Golding translates:

There from his quiver full of shafts two arrowes he did take
Of sundrie powres; tone causeth love the tother doth it slake.
That causeth love, is all of golde with point full sharpe and bryght,
That chaseth love, is blunt whose steale with leaden head is dyght.

(p. 11a)

As these lines are contained in the account of Apollo and
Daphne, they may well be the direct source. The idea is
also to be found in Spenser, *Colin Clout's Come Home
Again* 807, and in the emblem-books. An early mediæval
instance is found in the Old French *Fablel dou Dieu
d'Amours*, see W. A. Neilson, *Origins and Sources of the
Court of Love*, p. 42.

More significant than Shakespeare's conception of Cupid
is the use which he makes of the myth. Two facts are
immediately obvious, (1) that mentions of Cupid are very
rare after 1601 (only 5 in the authentic plays), and (2)
that in all but a few instances the references are of a playful character, that Cupid is not *seriously* regarded as a
divinity of love. Thus he is spoken of playfully as 'blind
bow-boy'; his arrow is called a 'butt-shaft,' etc. To
this usage Mids. furnishes a sharp contrast, especially
in such a passage as that in 2. 1. 155 ff., where Cupid
takes aim 'At a fair vestal throned in the west.' Perhaps
with the fairy mythology of the play a serious Cupid seemed
more in keeping.

The distribution of the allusions to Cupid by name is as
follows: Ven. 1; LLL 10; Mids. 8; Rom. 5 (half playful,
half serious); Merch. 2; Wiv. 2; Ado 9 (very playful);
As 2; Alls 2; Sonn. 2 (half playful); Oth. 1 (in a disparaging
sense); Lr. 1 (in Lear's mad raving); Troil. 5 (rather more
serious); Ant. 1 (as figure in pageant); Cymb. 2 (in one
instance the figure of andirons); Per. 1. Gent. has no mention of Cupid by name, but Love with attributes of Cupid 9
times, rather seriously. Love is similarly mentioned twice
in Rom. with a considerable degree of seriousness. The
phrase 'Saint Cupid' occurs twice in LLL, 4. 3. 366; 5. 2.
87 (cf. Chaucer's 'Seynt Venus,' *Wif of Bath's Prologue*
604).

4

Cyclops.—Hml. 2. 511; Tit. 4. 3. 46.

In the first passage the Cyclopes are forging Mars' armor. In *Æn.* 8. 426 they are engaged in making him a chariot and flying wheels at the time when Venus comes to beg a suit of armor for Æneas (cf. s. v. Vulcan). Tit. 4. 3. 47 refers to the size of the Cyclops. Polyphemus is described in *Æn.* 3. 655 seq.; *Met.* 13. 764 seq.

Cynthia.—Ven. 728; Rom. 3. 5. 20; Per. 2. 5. 11. See Diana.

Cytherea.—Pass. Pilg. 43; 73; Cymb. 2. 2. 14; Wint. 4. 4. 122; Shr. Ind. 2. 53. See Venus.

Dædalus (Icarus. Minos.)—H6A 4. 6. 55; 4. 7. 16; H6C 5. 6. 21.
(Minotaur.)—H6A 5. 3. 189.

Only in H6A and C is the Cretan story alluded to. Talbot, leading his brave son into danger, compares himself to Dædalus and his son to Icarus:

> And in that sea of blood my boy did drench
> His over-mounting spirit, and there died,
> My Icarus, my blossom, in his pride.

In H6C the King finds himself in a similar position. He says to Gloucester (Richard):

> I, Dædalus; my poor boy Icarus;
> Thy father, Minos that denied our course;
> The sun that sear'd the wings of my sweet boy
> Thy brother Edward, and thyself the sea
> Whose envious gulf did swallow up his life.

The story is told at length in *Met.* 8. 183-235.

The allusion to the Minotaur is much less detailed. Suffolk, tempted to enter a dangerous intrigue, says to himself:

> Thou mayst not wander in that labyrinth;
> There Minotaurs and ugly treasons lurk.

This may perhaps be referred to *Met.* 8. 152 seq., though neither the word 'labyrinth' nor the name 'Minotaur' appears. Golding, however, has the latter (p. 105a). In *Æn.* 6. 26 the story is also touched on, and the name Minotaur mentioned. Both names are mentioned in North's Plutarch, *Theseus,* p. 49.

Danae (?).—Rom. 1. 1. 220. See Jupiter.

Daphne.—Mids. 2. 1. 231; Troil. 1. 1. 101; Shr. Ind. 2. 61. See
   Apollo.

Destiny, Destinies.—See Fate.

Deucalion.—Cor. 2. 1. 102; Wint. 4. 4. 441; (Cæs. 1. 2. 152).

Deucalion is mentioned twice in plays with classical setting as equivalent to Noah, i. e. as the common ancestor of
the race, or as one standing in the dawn of history. Cf.
'Since before Noah was a sailor,' Tw. 3. 2. 18. The 'great
flood' of Cæs. 1. 2. 152 is probably Deucalion's. For the
story see *Met.* 1. 313 seq.

Diana.

It is as patroness and type of chastity that Shakespeare
most often alludes to Diana. These allusions, of which
there are sixteen in the authentic plays, cover the whole
range of Shakespeare's activity from Mids. to Cymb., and
are pretty evenly divided between tragedies and comedies,
but never occur in the histories. In this capacity, Diana is
antithetic to Cupid (or Venus). The antithesis is expressed
in Rom. 1. 1. 215; Ado 4. 1. 58; Alls 1. 3. 218; 2. 3. 80.
In Mids. 4. 1. 76,

> Dian's bud o'er Cupid's flower
> Hath such force and blessed power,

Steevens sees an allusion to the *Agnus Castus,* 'the virtue of
which is that he will keep man and woman chaste' (see the
Chaucerian *Flower and the Leaf* 472-5). The line is more
simply explained by Ado 4. 1. 58:

> You seem to me as Dian in her orb,
> As chaste as is the bud ere it be blown.

Still the context would seem to show that 'Cupid's flower'
is the 'love-in-idleness' of 2. 1. 168, and we not unnaturally

expect a particular flower to counteract its charm. It is noticeable that as patroness of chastity, Shakespeare mentions the divinity by only one name, Diana (or Dian).

Next in frequency are the allusions to Diana as the moon-goddess, or oftener by metonymy as the moon itself; but these allusions are largely confined to the earlier works: Ven. 725, 728; LLL 4. 2. 35 ff.; Gent. 4. 2. 100; Mids. 1. 1. 209; 3. 2. 53; Rom. 2. 2. 4; 3. 5. 20; Merch. 5. 1. 109; H4A 1. 2. 29. (Perhaps also Ado 5. 3. 12; Cor. 5. 3. 67.) In this aspect, and in this aspect alone in the authentic plays, she receives her alternate names, Phœbe and Cynthia. Holofernes in LLL calls her also Luna and Dictynna. This latter title is found in Ovid, *Met.* 2. 441; 5. 619; *Fasti* 6. 755. In the first of these passages it is preserved by Golding; in the second he substitutes 'Diana.' In Mids. 3. 2. 53 the moon is spoken of as sister to the sun. If authority is needed for this relationship, the reader is referred to *Met.* 2. 454.

Diana as the huntress, frequenter of groves, the center of a band of nymphs, appears but little in the authentic plays, and in them her bow is not mentioned at all. The earliest allusion is in H4A 1. 2. 29. Others are Ado 5. 3. 12(?); Alls 1. 3. 119(?); Cymb. 2. 3. 74; 2. 4. 82. Of these, only the passages in Cymb. are clear allusions. The first of these, the picture of 'chaste Dian bathing' in Imogen's chamber, may refer to the story of Callisto, *Met.* 2. 401-465, or to that of Actæon, *Met.* 3. 138-252, or perhaps Shakespeare had some actual painting or tapestry in mind. The phrase 'virgin knight' of Diana in Ado 5. 3. 12 and the similar use of 'knight' in Alls 1. 3. 119 suggest Spenser, but in Golding, p. 23b, Nonacris is called a 'Knyght of Phebes troope.' We may notice, too, that it is Diana as goddess of the groves who gives her name Titania to the queen of fairies in Mids. See *Met.* 3. 173 (the story of Actæon) and 6. 346. It has been noticed that in Golding's translation the name Titania does not occur.

In the doubtful plays, however, the allusions are more explicit. Thus in H6C 4. 8. 21:

> Like to his island girt in with the ocean,
> Or modest Dian circled with her nymphs,

we recognize an echo of the 'curcumfusæque Dianam corporibus texere suis' of *Met*. 3. 180-181, where the nymphs crowd around Diana at the approach of Actæon. (Cf. also *F. Q.* 3. 6. 19.) Again in Tit. 1. 1. 316:

> That like the stately Phœbe 'mongst her nymphs
> Dost overshine the gallant'st dames of Rome

we have the 'Tamen altior illis Ipsa dea est, colloque tenus supereminet omnes' of *Met*. 3. 181-182, or the similar description in *Æn*. 1. 501 seq. See also Shr. 2. 1. 260 ff.

'I will weep for nothing like Diana in the fountain,' As 4. 1. 154. Halliwell says that a weeping Diana was a common figure in Elizabethan fountains. But why is Diana represented as weeping?

Among the many allusions to Diana in Per. we have in 5. 1. 249 a mention of her silver bow, and a few lines farther (251) she is called 'Celestial Dian, goddess argentine.' The latter epithet may have been suggested by 'argentea Cynthia' of Ovid, *Her*. 18. 71.

In As 3. 2. 2 Orlando appeals to the 'thrice-crowned queen of night,' alluding to her threefold character as Hecate, Diana, Luna. Though the phrase 'thrice-crowned' seems to have no exact classical equivalent, we find 'Per triplicis vultus arcanaque sacra Dianæ' in Ovid, *Her*. 12. 79, and 'diva triformis,' *Met*. 7. 177, and in *Æn*. 4. 511 'tria virginis ora Dianæ.' Singer has noticed that Chapman speaks of her 'triple forehead' in *Hymnus in Cynthiam* (1594).

As an infernal deity, HECATE, she is alluded to in the following passages: Mids. 5. 1. 391; Hml. 3. 2. 269; Mcb. 2. 1. 52; 3. 2. 41; 3. 5; Lr. 1. 1. 112; H6A 3. 2. 64. The ancients thought of Hecate first as a moon-goddess, then as a divinity of the infernal regions, and, lastly, as a natural development of these two ideas, as patroness of witches. That Shakespeare was acquainted with all of these conceptions, is shown by one of the witch scenes in Mcb. (3. 5), where she appears as queen of witches, and in the course of her long speech suggests her infernal character by an invitation to meet her 'at the pit of Acheron,' and her connection with the moon by the lines:

> Upon the corner of the moon
> There hangs a vaporous drop profound;
> I'll catch it ere it comes to ground.

Her connection with witchcraft, though found in many Latin authors (notably Seneca, *Medea*), is perhaps to be traced to the incantation of Medea in *Met.* 7. 1-293. Thus in translating *Met.* 7. 74-75, Golding reads:

> She went me to an altar that was dedicate of olde
> To Perseys daughter Hecate (of whom the witches holde
> As of their goddesse).

The passage in parentheses is Golding's interpolation. This conception of Hecate as mistress of witchcraft is further illustrated by Hml. 3. 2. 269, Mcb. 2. 1. 52, and perhaps Lr. 2. 1. 41 where Edgar is described as standing in the dark,

> his sharp sword out,
> Mumbling of wicked charms, conjuring the moon
> To stand auspicious mistress.

In H6A 3. 2. 64, the supposed witch, Jeanne d'Arc, is called by Talbot a 'railing Hecate.'

There are two passages in which Hecate is thought of merely as representative of darkness or night. The three notions of Hecate mentioned above are all suggestive of darkness, and already in Ovid we find the name of Hecate associated with that of Nox. For example, in the enchantment of Circe in *Met.* 14. 403-405 we read:

> Illa nocens spargit virus sucosque veneni,
> Et Noctem Noctisque deos Ereboque Chaoque
> Convocat, et longis Hecaten ululatibus orat.

That this association was present to Shakespeare's mind also may be shown from Lear's solemn adjuration (1. 1. 112):

> For, by the sacred radiance of the sun,
> The mysteries of Hecate, and the night.

From close association it is only a short step to confusion
and virtual identification, and this step has, I think, been
taken in the following passage of Mcb. (3. 2. 40-43) :

> Ere the bat hath flown
> His cloister'd flight, ere to black Hecate's summons
> The shard-borne beetle with his drowsy hums
> Hath rung night's yawning peal, there shall be done
> A deed of dreadful note.

There is no reference here to the witch-queen of the *dramatis
personæ;* in plain prose, Macbeth means to say that before
the night is over Banquo and Fleance will have been murdered. It has puzzled the commentators to explain why
Hecate's name is introduced at all, and why she should be
called 'black,' an epithet obviously inappropriate for a moon-
divinity. It is possible, of course, to consider 'black' as
equivalent to malignant, as in the phrases 'black magician'
(R3. 1. 2. 34), and 'black fate' (Rom. 3. 1. 124) ; but this
still leaves the first question unanswered. All difficulty is
removed if we admit that Shakespeare is using the name
Hecate as equivalent with Night. There is one more passage which seems to confirm this view in the closing scene
of Mids. :

> Now it is the time of night,
>   That the graves, all gaping wide,
> Every one lets forth his sprite,
>   In the church-way paths to glide:
> And we fairies, that do run
>   By the triple Hecate's team,
> From the presence of the sun,
>   Following darkness like a dream,
> Now are frolic.

If Hecate is the moon, with what appropriateness can those
who run by her team be said to follow darkness ! If on the
other hand, Hecate means only night, or darkness, the incon-
sistency immediately disappears.

But what is the team of triple Hecate by which the fairies
run? Ovid mentions no team as belonging to Hecate, but

he does tell us in *Met.* 7. 219 (so Seneca, *Med.* 1023; cf. Euripides, *Med.* 1321) that Medea's prayer to Hecate is answered by the descent of a dragon-drawn car in which Medea is carried aloft, and Shakespeare's contemporaries, if not Shakespeare himself, ascribed a dragon-yoke to Hecate. (Cf. Marlowe, *Hero and Leander* 1. 103; Drayton, *The Man in the Moon* (about 100 lines from the end); Milton, *Il Penseroso* 59, and *In Obitum Præsulis Eliensis* 56.) These facts seem to warrant us in asserting that 'triple Hecate's team' is a team of dragons, and that the phrase is the exact equivalent of 'night's swift dragons,' in Mids. 3. 2. 379. (Cf. s. v. Night.) Golding uses the phrase 'triple Hecate' twice in his translation of *Met.* 7, as equivalent to the 'triformis deæ' of ll. 94-5, and the 'triceps Hecate' of l. 194.

With the lines from Lr. (1. 1. 112) quoted above we may compare Dido's lament in *Æn.* 4. 607-609:

> Sol, qui terrarum flammis opera omnia lustras,
> Tuque harum interpres curarum et conscia Iuno
> Nocturnisque Hecate triviis ululata per urbes.

Dictynna.—LLL 4. 2. 37, 38. See Diana.

Dido.—Mids. 1. 1. 173; Rom. 2. 4. 43; Merch. 5. 1. 10; Hml. 2. 2. 468; Ant. 4. 14. 53; Tp. 2. 1. 76, 78, 81, 100, 101; Tit. 2. 3. 22; 5. 3. 82; H6B 3. 2. 117; Shr. 1. 1. 159.

The story of Dido in *Æn.* I-IV must have been familiar to Shakespeare from his boyhood. The allusions are numerous and substantially accurate. Twice the allusion is to the story of Troy's fall related by Æneas at her request, *Æn.* 2. (Hml. 2. 2. 468; Tit. 5. 3. 82). In *Æn.* 1. 720-722 Cupid, having assumed the form of Ascanius, is fondled by Dido, and 'little by little essays to blot out the remembrance of Sichæus, and with a living passion to preoccupy a heart long dead to love.' This would seem to be the authority for H6B 3. 2. 117:

> To sit and witch me, as Ascanius did
> When he to madding Dido would unfold
> His father's acts commenced in burning Troy.

In Shr. 1. 1. 159 we have mention of Anna as her confidante. Cf. *Æn.* 4. passim. The episode in the cave, where she and Æneas took refuge during a thunder storm (*Æn.* 4. 165-172) is mentioned in Tit. 2. 3. 22.

There are two allusions to her abandonment by Æneas, which represent different versions of the story. In Mids. 1. 1. 173:

> And by that fire which burn'd the Carthage queen,
> When the false Troyan under sail was seen,

we have a reference to *Æn.* 5. 1. seq. The lines in Merch. 5. 1. 10 present more difficulty:

> In such a night (i. e. moonlight)
> Stood Dido with a willow in her hand
> Upon the wild sea banks and waft her love
> To come again to Carthage.

Matthew Arnold in his *Celtic Literature,* p. 128, has noticed the peculiarly modern, unclassical tone of this picture. There is nothing to correspond to it in Vergil, though Dido's letter to Æneas in Ovid, *Her.* 7, contains several references to the wild sea, and is a passionate appeal for his return. The true source for the lines is to be found, Malone suggested, in Chaucer's *Legend of Good Women* 2189 ff.:

> And to the stronde bar-fot faste she wente,
> And cryed, 'Theseus! myn herte swete!'
> .   .   .   .
> The holwe rokkes answerde her again;
> No man she saw, and yit shyned the mone,
> And hye upon a rokke she wente sone,
> And saw his barge sailing in the see.
> .   .   .   .   .   .
> Her kerchef on a pole up stikked she,
> Ascaunce that he sholde hit wel y-see,
> And him remembre that she was behinde,
> And turne again, and on the stronde her finde.

Chaucer's lines are in turn closely modelled on Ovid, *Her.* 10, and there is no reason to suppose that Shakespeare had Chaucer in mind rather than Ovid. In either case, Shakespeare has changed the application from Ariadne to Dido.

In Ant. 4. 14. 53 Antony says that when he and Cleopatra come to Elysium,

> Dido and her Æneas shall want troops,
> And all the haunt be ours.

i. e. Dido and Æneas will no longer be the most conspicuous pair of lovers.   The allusions in Rom. and Tp. are playful.

Diomed.—H6C 4. 2. 19; Troil. passim.

His participation in the capture of Rhesus' steeds is mentioned in H6C (see Ulysses).   The conception of the character in Troil. is taken from Caxton and from Chaucer.

Dis.—Tp. 4. 1. 89; Wint. 4. 4. 118.   See Pluto.

Echo.—Rom. 2. 2. 162; Tit. 2. 3. 17.

In the balcony scene of Rom., Juliet says:

> Else would I tear the cave where Echo lies,
> And make her airy tongue more hoarse than mine,
> With repetition of my Romeo's name.

The story of Echo and Narcissus is told in *Met.* 3. 339 seq. In ll. 393-94 we read:

> Spreta *latet* silvis, pudibundaque frondibus ora
> Protegit, et solis ex illo vivit in *antris.*

and in 397-98:

> Et in *aera* sucus
> Corporis omnis abit.

In Tit. the poet speaks of 'the babbling echo.' This is the '*vocalis* nymphe' of *Met.* 3. 357, rendered by Golding (p. 36b),

> A babling Nymph that Echo hight.

Shakespeare, though acquainted with the story of Narcissus, never connects him with Echo.

Elysium.—See Hades.

Enceladus.—Tit. 4. 2. 93.

Enceladus is the giant who, warring against the gods, was struck by a thunderbolt, and imprisoned under Ætna. (*Æn.* 3. 578,) He is mentioned with Hercules and Mars as a mighty man of war.

Erebus.—See Hades.

Europa.—H4B 2. 2. 193; Wiv. 5. 5. 4; Ado 5. 4. 45; Troil. 5. 1. 59; Wint. 4. 4. 27; Shr. 1. 1. 174. See Jupiter.

Fame (Report, Rumor).

Under these names is personified that mysterious power which seems to disseminate the news of any great occurrence, mingling truth with falsehood. Most vivid is the personification in H4B, Induction, where Rumor enters, 'painted full of tongues,' and gives a lying report of the battle of Shrewsbury. For this the ultimate source is to be found in *Æn.* 4. 174-188, where Vergil describes Rumor as 'a monster frightful, huge; who, for every feather of her body, has as many wakeful eyes beneath, (wondrous to tell) as many loud tongues and mouths, as many ears that she pricks up to listen.' The conception is, of course, a very common one among Shakespeare's contemporaries: cf. the paraphrase of the Vergilian passage in Jonson's *Poetaster* 5. 1. Similar, though much less elaborate, are the 'Lady Fame' of Ado 2. 1. 221, 'my gossip Report' of Merch. 3. 1. 7, and also K. J. 4. 2. 123; Per. 3. prol. 22. An explicit allusion to the Ovidian 'house of Fame' (*Met.* 12. 39-63) is found in Tit. 2. 1. 126. Though,

> The palace full of tongues, of eyes, and ears,

seems to suggest *Æn.* 4. 174-188 quoted above. Cf. also Chaucer's *Hous of Fame.* Not to be confused with Fame in this sense are the numerous personifications of fame as glory, reputation—such, for example, as Troil. 3. 3. 210; 4. 5. 143.

Fate (Destiny, Destinies, Necessity).

Shakespeare's conception of Fate or Destiny is philosophical rather than mythological. An irresistible power governing the lives of men, overruling their wishes and desires (Mids. 3. 2. 92; Wint. 4. 4. 46), and even thwarting Nature (Ven. 733); not necessarily hostile, but 'sharp' and inexorable (Ant. 4. 14. 135; Ado 4. 1. 116)—this is Shakespeare's conception of Fate in all periods of his work. It is part of Macbeth's curse that he 'shall spurn fate,' thus opposing himself to the laws of the universe. There is no attempt to theologize about it. It is neither identified with nor opposed to divine omnipotence; the exact relation between fate and man's free will is nowhere definitely fixed. To Shakespeare, Fate stands for an intervention, mysterious, inexplicable. From Ariel's mouth we learn (Tp. 3. 3. 53) that the forces of nature are but an instrument for performing the decrees of Destiny.

Shakespeare is familiar with the late Roman conception of the three fates expressed in the *Latin Anthology* 1. 792, ed. Riese:

> Tres sunt fatales quæ ducunt fila sorores:
> Clotho colum baiulat, Lachesis trahit, Atropos occat.

That these verses were common in Shakespeare's time we know on the authority of ' E. K.' in his gloss on Spenser's *Shep. Cal. November:* 'The fatall sisters, Clotho, Lachesis, and Atropos, daughters of Herebus and the Nighte, whom the Poetes fayne to spinne the life of man, as it were a long threde, which they drawe out in length, till his fatal howre and timely death be come; but if by other casualtie his dayes be abridged, then one of them, that is, Atropos, is sayde to have cut the threde in twain. Hereof commeth a common verse. "Clotho colum, etc."' Cf. also Peele's *Arraignment of Paris* 5. 1. 128. But this mythological treatment occurs *seriously* only three times, K. J. 4. 2. 91; R2. 1. 2. 15; Per. 1. 2. 108. It is parodied twice by Pistol, (H4B 2. 4. 213, where Atropos is named, and H5. 5. 1. 21) in the most absurd way, and again in the play of the mechanicals in Mids. (5. 1. 290, 343) where Shakespeare is laughing at an old play. In Merch. 2. 2. 65 Launcelot Gobbo refers to 'the Sisters Three and such branches of learning.' Perhaps Shakespeare is satirizing the frequent references to the Fates in such dramas as those of Peele.

Flora.—Wint. 4. 4. 2.

Florizel calls Perdita 'no shepherdess, but Flora Peering in April's front.' Shakespeare has taken this over from *Dorastus and Fawnia,* the main source of Wint.: 'She defended her face from the heat of the sunne with no other vale, but with a garland made of bowes and flowers; which attire became her so gallantly as shee seemed to bee the Goddesse Flora her selfe for beauty.' *Shak. Lib.* Pt. I. Vol. 4. p. 49.

Fortune.

Fortune, a personification, half mythological, half philosophical, of the unstable, irresponsible power which seems to govern the happiness of men, furthering or defeating their plans, is to be found frequently in Shakespeare. To the Greeks and Romans she was a divinity, to Dante one of the divine Intelligences (*Inf.* 7. 67 ff.), to Shakespeare a half-personified abstraction with many of the attributes of the Roman Fortuna. Shakespeare's treatment of her is to be compared with his treatment of Fate, a conception which at times resembles closely that of Fortune, save that the interpositions of Fate imply a preordained plan, while those of Fortune are purely capricious. At least half of the passages in which fortune is mentioned are general, indefinite, and without significance. At times she is regarded as a hostile, at times a beneficent power, at times her changeableness is the point emphasized. In the remaining instances we find epithets or attributes which furnish a point of attack. While it is impossible to prove any definite indebtedness, it is possible to say which of these conceptions are classic and which are not.

Classical art represented Fortuna most commonly as a
woman standing, in the left hand holding a cornucopia, in
the right a ship's rudder resting on a globe—the cornucopia
representing her favors, the rudder her directing power,
and the globe her changeableness.   On her head is a high
helmet.   (See Roscher, s. v. Fortuna.)   Such representations with various modifications may well have been familiar
to Shakespeare in tapestries or in emblem-books.   Thus
H4B 4. 4. 103,

> Will Fortune never come with both hands full,

is suggestive of the cornucopia in one hand only.   And in
Cymb. 4. 3. 46,

> Fortune brings in some boats that are not steer'd,

there is possible allusion to the rudder.   In Hml. 2. 2. 233,

> Happy, in that we are not over-happy;
> On Fortune's cap we are not the very button,

the allusion is less convincing.   The globe or wheel of Fortune early found its way into literature.   In Ovid, *Pont.*
2. 3. 56, she is spoken of as 'Stans in orbe Dea.'   Other passages are Cicero, *Pis.* 10, and without direct mention of Fortune, Horace, *Od.* 3. 10. 10.   In mediæval literature the
wheel is a common attribute.   For illustration the reader
is referred to Dante, *Inf.* 7. 218; Marie de France, *Lais,
Guigemar* 538; *Cursor Mundi* 32719; Chaucer, *Fortune*
46; Gower, *Conf. Am.* 1. 2624.   With Shakespeare's contemporaries the idea is also familiar.   In Whitney's *Choice
of Emblems* (1586), p. 181, Occasion is represented as standing with her left foot resting on the hub of a wheel which
she is whirling about with her right foot.   Shakespeare's
allusions are as follows: Lucr. 952; H5. 3. 6. 28; As 1. 2.
33; Lr. 2. 2. 180; 5. 3. 174; Ant. 4. 15. 44; H6C 4. 3. 46.
In As and Ant. she is also spoken of as a 'housewife,' which
would seem to suggest that, either playfully or otherwise, the
wheel is thought of as a spinning-wheel.   It is quite probable
that Rosalind should make the error in sport; that Cleo-

patra should do so while Antony is dying seems less probable. In H5. 5. 1. 85 Pistol says:

> Doth Fortune play the huswife with me now,

which might suggest that in all three of these passages housewife = 'hussy, a light woman,' and that there is no thought whatever of the spinning-wheel. That Shakespeare understood the significance of the wheel is shown by Fluelen's dissertation to Pistol in H5. 3. 6. 34: 'She is painted also with a wheel, to signify to you, which is the moral of it, that she is turning, and inconstant, and mutability, and variation; and her foot, look you, is fixed upon a spherical stone, which rolls, and rolls, and rolls.'

In H5. 3. 6. 29; As 1. 2. 36, she is spoken of as blind. For this we have the authority of Cicero, *Læl.* 15, and Pliny, *N. H.* 2. 5. 7. She is also blind in Chaucer, *Fortune* 50. Classical authority for the phrase 'Lady Fortune,' As 2. 7. 16; Wint. 4. 4. 51; Per. 4. 4. 48; (cf. also K. J. 3. 1. 118) is to be found in the epithet 'domina' of Cicero, *Marcell.* 2. The phrase 'bountiful Fortune' of As 1. 2. 38; Tp. 1. 2. 178, finds a parallel in Statius, *Silv.* 6. 68.

Other conceptions seem distinctly modern. She is called 'strumpet' or 'whore' in K. J. 3. 1. 52; Hml. 2. 2. 240, 515; Mcb. 1. 2. 15; Lr. 2. 4. 52. Perhaps purely Elizabethan are Hml. 3. 1. 58:

> The slings and arrows of outrageous fortune,

and similar expressions in Tit. 2. 1. 2; Per. 3. 3. 6. So too we should consider the allegory of the Poet in Tim. (1. 1. 63 ff.):

> Sir, I have upon a high and pleasant hill
> Feign'd Fortune to be throned; etc.

In three passages, K. J. 3. 1. 52; Wiv. 3. 3. 69; As 1. 2. 40 ff., an antithesis is expressed between Fortune and Nature which is summed up by Rosalind in the words:

Fortune reigns in gifts of the world, not in the lineaments of Nature.

i. e. Fortune does not determine our physical appearance. (See Nature.)

In As 2. 7. 19 we have an allusion to the proverb 'Fortuna favet fatuis.'

Furies.—Err. 4. 2. 35; Mids. 5. 1. 289; R3. 1. 4. 57; H4B 5. 3. 110; Ado 1. 1. 193; Alls 5. 3. 261; Ant. 2. 5. 40; Tit. 5. 2. 82.

Shakespeare is quite ignorant of the Eumenides of the Greek tragedians, the personified stingings of conscience. Vergil mentions the Furies among the other infernal machinery of the sixth *Æneid*, and to Shakespeare they are merely fiends, or devils. Thus in R3 Clarence dreams that he has gone to hell, and that some one cried:

> Seize on him, Furies, take him to your torments.

Parolles in Alls mentions Satan, Limbo, and Furies together; and in Ado, Benedick says that Beatrice is '*possessed* with a fury.' In Err. the sheriff's officer is called 'A fiend, a fury, pitiless and rough.' More distinctly Vergilian is the allusion in Ant.:

> Thou shouldst come like a Fury crown'd with snakes.

Alecto is thus described in *Æn.* 7. 346. Pistol, in one of his ranting speeches, H4B 5. 5. 39, mentions 'fell Alecto's snake.'

Only in Tit. is there any thought of the Furies as avengers of crime, where Tamora, masquerading as Revenge, is addressed by Titus as 'dread Fury.' The identification of the furies with the fiends of the Christian hell is common to Shakespeare's contemporaries.

Ganymede.—As 1. 3. 127. See Jupiter.

Golden Age.—Lucr. 60; As 1. 1. 125; Tp. 2. 1. 168.

These are merely allusions. If a source is needed it may be found in *Met.* 1. 89 seq. The phrase 'golden world' in As is paralleled by Golding p. 188b.

Gorgon.—Mcb. 2. 3. 77; Ant. 2. 5. 116. See Perseus.

Hades. (*Under this head are discussed* **Erebus, Tartarus, Elysium**
and **Acheron, Cocytus, Lethe, Styx.**)

The name Hades is nowhere mentioned by Shakespeare,
and nowhere is any comprehensive description of it given.
His conception of the region, so far as it was at all definite,
must be gathered from his frequent use of the names mentioned above. *Æn.* 6 is, of course, the main ultimate source.

ErEBUS is mentioned three times: Merch. 5. 1. 87;
H4B 2. 4. 169; Cæs. 2. 1. 84. Originally Erebus is a personification of darkness (cf. Hesiod, *Theog.* 123), but even
in Homer it is used as a name for the lower regions (*Il.* 8.
368), and this is the sense in which, with one exception, it
is used by Vergil. The notion of darkness clings to it in
such passages as *Æn.* 4. 26; 6. 404, and Shakespeare uses
as epithets 'dim' and 'dark.' It is to him a type of darkness.
The Ovidian notion is similar, cf. *Met.* 10. 76; 14. 404. Pistol's use of the word in H4B has been referred by Malone
to a passage in Peele's *Battle of Alcazar* (1594), Act 4.

TARTARUS.—Err. 4. 2. 32; H5. 2. 2. 123; Tw. 2. 5. 225
(always in the form 'Tartar'). The location of Tartarus
within the infernal regions is not specified by Shakespeare.
The passage in Err., however, shows that he knew it to be
the worst part of hell. The ultimate source is *Æn.* 6. 548-
627. 'Vasty Tartar' of H5 may be referred to ll. 577-579:

> Tum Tartarus ipse
> Bis patet in præceps tantum, tenditque sub umbras,
> Quantus ad ætherium cæli suspectus Olympum.

The mention of *legions* a few lines below,

> And tell the legions 'I can never win,'

suggests a Biblical reminiscence.

'To the gates of Tartar, thou most excellent devil of wit'
in Tw. may be only another way of saying 'To hell-gate.'
The gate of Tartarus is, however, specifically mentioned by
Vergil in l. 552.

ELYSIUM.—Ven. 600; Gent. 2. 7. 38; H5. 4. 1. 291;
Tw. 1. 2. 4; Troil. 3. 2. 12; Ant. 4. 14. 51; Cymb. 5. 4. 97;

5

H6B 3. 2. 399; H6C 1. 2. 30. Elysium, the abode of the blest, is described in *Æn.* 6. 637-659. Most of Shakespeare's references are without significance, Elysium being equivalent to Paradise. Of more significance, however, are Troil., Ant., and Cymb. In Ant. we read:

> Stay for me:
> Where souls do couch on flowers, we'll hand in hand,

and in Troil.:

> O, be thou my Charon,
> And give me swift transportation to those fields
> Where I may wallow in the lily-beds
> Proposed for the deserver.
> (Spoken by Troilus to Pandar.)

Again in Cymb.:

> Poor shadows of Elysium, hence, and rest
> Upon your never-withering banks of flowers.

In each case, then, where Elysium is described the flowers are given chief prominence. Now Vergil, though mentioning 'the smiling lawns of happy groves' and 'the fragrant bay-trees,' and saying that the ghosts 'dwell in the shady woods, and haunt the couches that the river-banks afford, and the meadows that the fountains freshen,' does not mention any flowers; but in the Homeric Hades the spirits pass 'along the mead of asphodel,' *Od.* 11. 539, and the asphodel is a species of lily. (In *Æn.* 6. 883 Anchises says 'give me handfuls of lilies,' which implies that they grew in Vergil's Elysian Fields also.)

ACHERON.—Mids. 3. 2. 357; Mcb. 3. 5. 15; Tit. 4. 3. 44. Vergil's description of Acheron is not minute, and Shakespeare does not seem very sure what it is. Thus in Mcb. we have 'the pit of Acheron,' and in Tit. it is apparently a 'burning lake.' In Mids. the heaven is covered

> With drooping fog as black as Acheron.

Æn. 6. 107 is perhaps responsible for the last: 'Tenebrosa palus Acheronte refuso.' The phrase 'pit of Acheron' in

Mcb. is apparently applied by the witches to some tarn near the scene of the action.

COCYTUS.—Mentioned only in Tit. 2. 3. 236:

> As hateful as Cocytus' misty mouth.

Cocytus is mentioned by Vergil in *Æn.* 6. 323 et alibi.

LETHE.—R3. 4. 4. 250; H4B 5. 2. 72; Tw. 4. 1. 66; Hml. 1. 5. 33; Ant. 2. 1. 27; 2. 7. 114. The river of forgetfulness is described in *Æn.* 6. 703-723, but of course the idea is a familiar one. Twice Shakespeare uses the word as a synonym of forgetfulness:

> Let fancy still my sense in Lethe steep.

Tw. 4. 1. 66, also Ant. 2. 7. 114. Similar to this is the adjectival use in Ant. 2. 1. 27: 'a Lethe'd dulness.' The allusions in R3 and H4B would indicate that Shakespeare thinks of Lethe as 'washing' away or 'drowning' memory. In Vergil it is by drinking of the water that the souls win oblivion. But in the *Divine Comedy, Purg.* 31. 101, Beatrice *submerges* Dante in Lethe up to the head so that he may in that way swallow some of the water. The immersion is made more prominent than the drinking. Special difficulty is given by the passage in Hml.; the Ghost says to Hamlet:

> I find thee apt;
> And duller shouldst thou be than the fat weed
> That roots itself in ease on Lethe wharf,
> Wouldst thou not stir in this.

The editors give no satisfactory explanation. Tschischwitz says the 'fat weed' must be asphodel and quotes Lucian (Περὶ Πένθους 5) who speaks of asphodel in somewhat remote connection with Lethe. Steevens quotes an interesting parallel from Beaumont and Fletcher's *Humorous Lieutenant* 4. 3:

> This dull root, plucked from Lethe flood,
> Purges all pure thoughts and good.

Here the context shows that the 'dull root' has baleful magic powers. If Shakespeare had any particular plant in

mind, I think I can show that it is the poppy.   Both Ovid
and Vergil connect the poppy with Lethe.   Thus in describing the house of sleep, *Met.* 11. 602-605:

> Saxo tamen exit ab imo
> Rivus aquæ Lethes, per quem cum murmure labens
> Invitat somnos crepitantibus unda lapillis.
> Ante fores antri fecunda papavera florent;

and in *Met.* 7. 152 Jason sprinkles the dragon 'with the iuce
of certaine herbes from Lethey River sent,' which are of
soporific virtue.   Vergil speaks of 'Lethæa papavera' in
Georg. 4. 545, and 'Lethæo perfusa papavera somno' in
Georg. 1. 78.   If Shakespeare *was* thinking of the poppy,
then 'fat weed' would mean a weed which makes 'fat' or
'dull.'   For similar prolepsis cf. 'The *insane root* That takes
the reason prisoner,' Mcb. 1. 3. 84, or 'Not poppy, nor man-
dragora, Nor all the *drowsy syrups* of the east.'   Oth. 3. 3.
330.   ('Wharf' = shore, bank, the only sense in which
Shakespeare uses the word.)

    STYX.—R3. 1. 4. 46; Troil. 3. 2. 10; 5. 4. 20; Tit. 1.
1. 88; 2. 1. 135.   In Troil. 3 we read:

> No, Pandarus; I stalk about her door,
> Like a strange soul upon the Stygian banks
> Staying for waftage.   O, be thou my Charon;

and in Tit. 1:

> Why suffer'st thou thy sons, unburied yet,
> To hover on the dreadful shore of Styx?

In R3:

> (My soul) pass'd, methought, the melancholy flood,
> With that grim ferryman which poets write of.

The conception expressed in these passages is found in *Æn.*
6. 295-336.   The Latin 'Per Styga, per manes vehor' of
Tit. 2. 1. 135 is an inexact quotation of Seneca, *Hippolytus*
1180:

> Per Styga, per amnes igneos amens sequar,

spoken by Phædra longing to see the face of her loved
Hippolytus.

Harpy.—Ado 2. 1. 279; Tp. 3. 3. 53 dir., 83; Per. 4. 3. 46.

Of these passages the most important is the stage direction in Tp.: 'Thunder and lightning. Enter Ariel, like a harpy; claps his wings upon the table; and, with a quaint device, the banquet vanishes.' This is evidently suggested by *Æn.* 3. 219-267, where the Harpies defile the banquet of Æneas and his companions. The clapping of Ariel's wings is the 'magnis quatiunt clangoribus alas' of l. 226. The thunder and lightning is that which accompanies many exhibitions of the supernatural in Shakespeare.

In Ado, Benedick playfully calls Beatrice a harpy, implying that she is both beautiful and malignant.

The allusion in Per. is explained by *Æn.* 3. 217. Steevens thinks that 'Harpier' of Mcb. 4. 1. 3 is a spelling of Harpy.

Hecate.—See Diana.

Hector.—LLL 5. 2. passim; Lucr. 1430; 1486; Wiv. 1. 3. 12; 2. 3. 35; Ado 2. 3. 196; Ant. 4. 8. 7; Cor. 1. 3. 44; 1. 8. 11; Tit. 4. 1. 88; H6A 2. 3. 20; H6C 2. 1. 51; 4. 8. 25; Troil. passim.

The character of Hector in Troil. is a very pleasing one; he is brave and honorable; his 'patience is as a virtue fixed,' 1. 2. 4; he is generous, and ready to spare a fallen enemy, 4. 5. 189. This is the conception of Caxton in every detail. (See p. 543, etc.)

In Lucr. he marches out to field, and later 'faints.' In Cor. he is the son of Hecuba, and a soldier. In all the other allusions he is a mere name, a type of valor and martial prowess.

Four times, Lucr. 1430; Tit. 4. 1. 88; H6C 2. 1. 51; 4. 8. 25, he is called 'the hope of Troy.' Æneas addresses him in *Æn.* 2. 281 as

> O lux Dardaniæ! spes O fidissima Teucrum!

Hecuba.—Lucr. 1447; 1485; Hml. 2. 2. 523, 584; Cor. 1. 3. 43; Cymb. 4. 2. 313; Tit. 1. 1. 136; 4. 1. 20.

In Lucr. and Hml. the reference is to Hecuba's grief at the death of Priam (see Priam). In Cor. she is mentioned

as the mother of Hector.   The remaining references are to
her fortunes after the fall of Troy, as contained in *Met.* 13.
439-575.   Carried into captivity by the victor Greeks, she
witnesses the death of her daughter Polyxena, and dis-
covers that her son Polydorus has been treacherously murdered by the Thracian king, Polymnestor.   Mad with sorrow,
she beguiles Polymnestor into a secret place and tears out
his eyes, and, while railing at the Greeks, is metamorphosed
into a bitch.   In Cymb., Imogen, seeing what she supposes
to be the murdered body of her husband, says to Pisanio:

> All curses madded Hecuba gave the Greeks,
> And mine to boot, be darted on thee!

In Tit. 4. the allusion is also to her 'running mad for sorrow.'
In Tit. 1. we read:

> The self-same gods that arm'd the Queen of Troy
> With opportunity of sharp revenge
> Upon the Thracian tyrant in his. tent.

This agrees with Ovid's story except that there the revenge
is taken not in Polymnestor's tent, but in a secret place to
which Hecuba has lured him (*in secreta,* l. 555).   In the
Hecuba of Euripides the scene takes place not in Polymnestor's tent, but in Hecuba's.   It is not impossible that the
story of Jael and Sisera might have influenced the author's
memory.   Could he perhaps have misread the following
lines of Golding (p. 168a and b):

> Queene Hecubee . . . . . too Polymnestor went
> The cursed murtherer, and desyrde his presence too thent ent
> Too shew too him a masse of gold (so made shee hir pretence)
> Which for hir lyttle Polydore was hyd not farre from thence.
> The Thracian king beleeving hir, as eager of the pray,
> Went with hir too a secret place.

In the edition of 1575, which I have used, the phrase
'thentent' (= the entent) is printed as above.   It seems to
me not inconceivable that it should be misread 'the tent,'
a substitution which would make good enough sense.

Helen.—Mids. 5. 1. 11; 5. 1. 200; Lucr. 1369, 1471; Rom. 2. 4. 44; H4B 5. 5. 35; As 3. 2. 153; Alls 1. 3. 74; Sonn. 53. 7; H6C 2. 2. 146; Shr. 1. 2. 244; Troil. passim.

Helen is a type of beauty, Mids. 5. 1. 11; Rom.; As; Sonn.; a type of falseness, As; H6C. She is mentioned as causing the Trojan war in Lucr. and Alls. In Shr. she is called 'fair Leda's daughter,' and is said to have had a thousand wooers. Paris addresses her as 'Ledæa' in the first line of his epistle to her, *Her.* 15. 1, and in the course of this and the following epistle the story of her mother is adverted to. In *Her.* 16. 104 she boasts of her thousand suitors. In Mids. 5. 1. 200 she is a type of fidelity, but the coupling of her name with that of 'Limander' shows that the mechanicals have confused her with Hero.

I shall not attempt here a discussion of the Helen of Troil.

Hercules (Alcides).

If Shakespeare's allusions to Hercules are extraordinarily numerous, his definite knowledge of the myth is exceedingly scanty. This knowledge consists: first, of general impressions gathered from conversation and miscellaneous reading; second, of more accurate knowledge gained from Ovid's incomplete version of the myth, and possibly from the English translation of Seneca.

Thus a large proportion of the allusions refer to Hercules merely as a type of valor and strength—'as valiant as Hercules,' 'as strong as Hercules.' 'To see great Hercules whipping a gig,' LLL 4. 3. 167, is an example of incongruity. When in As 1. 2. 222 Rosalind says to Orlando about to wrestle with Charles: 'Now Hercules be thy speed, young man,' she may have been thinking of the wrestling bout between Hercules and Achelous, *Met.* 9. 31 seq.

The twelve labors are referred to in a general way in Ado 2. 1. 380; Cor. 4. 1. 17; Shr. 1. 2. 257; that they were imposed by Juno seems to be implied by Alls 3. 4. 13, but there is no allusion to Eurystheus, nor to the reason for their imposition. Of the labors only four are alluded to in detail.

(1) *The Nemean lion* is referred to in LLL 4. 1. 90;
Hml. 1. 4. 83 as a type of ferocity. In K. J. 2. 1. 144
Alcides is spoken of as wearing a lion's skin (a fact Shakespeare might have learned from *Met.* 9. 113, or from pictorial representations). But the killing of the lion is not
referred to, unless humorously in Bottom's assertion: 'I
could play Ercles rarely, or a part to tear a cat in.' Mids.
1. 2. 31.

(2) *The Hydra* is mentioned or alluded to six times, but
never with any reference to Hercules. Thus we have 'as
many mouths as Hydra,' Oth. 2. 3. 308; 'Hydra-headed
wilfulness,' H5. 1. 1. 35; Hydra as a name for the many-
headed mob, Cor. 3. 1. 93 (and by allusion H4B Ind. 18) ;
'They grow like Hydra's heads,' H4A 5. 4. 25; and in
H4B 4. 2. 38:

> Whereon this Hydra son of war is born;
> Whose dangerous eyes may well be charm'd asleep
> With grant of our most just and right desires.

where there is, apparently, confusion with the story of Argus.
The Hydra is described in *Met.* 9. 70 seq.

(3) *The apples of the Hesperides.* Shakespeare's acquaintance with this labor is not very accurate. In LLL 4. 3. 340
we read:

> For valor, is not Love a Hercules,
> Still climbing trees in the Hesperides?

It has been noticed that here and in Per. 1. 1. 27 'the Hesperides' is considered the name of the garden, whereas the
Hesperides were really the custodians of the garden. Moreover in LLL and in Cor. 4. 6. 99 Hercules gathers the fruit
himself; while, according to the myth, he sent Atlas to do
it for him. It was during Atlas' errand that Hercules bore
his burden for him. Hamlet asks (2. 2. 378), 'Do the boys
(players) carry it away?' 'Ay, that they do, my lord;'
Rosencrantz answers, 'Hercules and his load too.' As
Steevens suggested, this is doubtless an allusion to the figure
of Hercules bearing the earth, which was the sign of the

Globe theatre. The dragon which guarded the apples is mentioned in Per.

(4) *The capture of Cerberus.* In the Masque of the Nine Worthies, LLL 5. 2. 592, the pedant, Holofernes, says:

> Great Hercules is presented by this imp,
> Whose club kill'd Cerberus, that three-headed canis.

Holofernes is, of course, wrong. Hercules dragged Cerberus up to the light (see *Met.* 7. 415), but sent him back alive.

In the same masque, LLL 5. 1. 41 ff.; 5. 2. 595, Moth presents Hercules strangling serpents. The incident might have been learned from Ovid, *Her.* 9. 21-22 or *Met.* 9. 67, which Golding translates: 'It is my cradle game To vanquish snakes.'

In Merch. 3. 2. 55 Portia refers in detail to the deliverance of Hesione (*Met.* 11. 199 seq.). In Ovid there is no hint of the Dardanian wives who stand aloof,

> With bleared visages, come forth to view
> The issue of the exploit;

but in Ovid's account of the similar adventure of Andromeda, *Met.* 4. 663 seq., her father and mother stand weeping.

Hercules in love with Omphale is mentioned in LLL 1. 2. 69, and probably also in Ado 2. 1. 261; 3. 3. 145. The last passage suggests that the subject was a favorite one in tapestry. Shakespeare may have been familiar with Ovid, *Her.* 9, though Omphale is not mentioned by name.

The attempt made by the Centaur Nessus to ravish Deianira (*Met.* 9. 101 seq.) is alluded to in Alls 4. 3. 283, and the poisoned Nessus-shirt in Ant. 4. 12. 43, and probably also in As 2. 3. 14, 15. As to Hercules' death, Shakespeare is fairly explicit. He twice refers to the page Lichas, who was thrown far into the air by the enraged hero, Merch. 2. 1. 32; Ant. 4. 12. 45, a detail which may have been learned from *Met.* 9. 217-18:

> terque quaterque rotatum
> Mittit in Euboicas tormento fortius undas;

but the phrase in Ant., 'Let me lodge Lichas on the horns of the moon,' seems nearer to the Senecan account of *Herc. Œtæus*, 815-822:

> *In astra* missus fertur, et nubes vago
> Spargit cruore.

That Shakespeare may have known this drama of Seneca in Studley's translation is suggested by a passage in Mids. I. 2. 31-43. Bottom says: 'I could play Ercles rarely,' and as proof of his ability quotes:

> The raging rocks
> And shivering shocks
> Shall break the locks
> Of prison gates. etc.

In the Senecan drama, 'Hercles,' as Studley calls him, recounts his own exploits in bad verse with excessive use of alliteration.

For Hercules' battle with the Centaurs see s. v. Centaurs.

Hermes.—H5. 3. 7. 19. See Mercury.

Hero and Leander.—Mids. 5. 1. 199; Gent. 1. 1. 22; 3. 1. 119; Rom. 2. 4. 44; Ado 5. 2. 30; As 4. 1. 100.

Marlowe's *Hero and Leander* was entered on the Stat. Reg. in 1593, published in 1598 (two sestiads), and republished with continuation by Chapman in 1600. This makes it unlikely that the first four of the above citations were drawn from the popular poem. In As (1600) Shakespeare quotes a line from the poem, so that the references in As and Ado (1599-1600) may well be attributed to Marlowe. In Gent. 1,

> *Pro.* Upon some book I love I'll pray for thee.

> *Val.* That's on some shallow story of deep love:
> How young Leander cross'd the Hellespont,

the allusion must be to Musæus. There were numerous Latin translations, and in 1544 a French translation by Clement Marot. None of the allusions is explicit enough

Icarus.—See Dædalus.

Ilium (Ilion).—(Ilium) Hml. 2. 2. 496; Troil. 1. 1. 104; 1. 2. 46,
  50, 194; (Ilion) LLL 5. 2. 658; Troil. 2. 2. 109; 4. 4. 118;
  4. 5. 112, 216; 5. 8. 11.

The name Ilium (Greek, Ilion) is properly a mere poetical equivalent of Troy, as in *Æn.* 2. 624-25:

> Tum vero omne mihi visum considere in ignes
> Ilium, et ex imo verti Neptunia Troia.

In this significance the form Ilion seems to be used by
Shakespeare; compare

> Troy must not be, nor goodly Ilion stand.
> > Troil. 2. 2. 109.
> So, Ilion, fall thou next! now, Troy, sink down!
> > Troil. 5. 8. 11.

and in LLL Hector is called 'heir of Ilion.'   But in all the
cases in which the form Ilium is used, the context shows
that Shakespeare means by it not the city, but Priam's
castle, the citadel of the town.   Thus in Troil. 1. 1. 104 we
read:

> Between our Ilium and where she resides,

i. e. Cressida's house in Troy; and in 1. 2. 46:

> When were you at Ilium?—This morning, uncle.

So too in Hml. 'senseless Ilium' is the palace (cf. Priam).
It is in this latter sense that Caxton uses the word Ylion:
'In the moste apparaunt place of the cyte upon a roche the
king pryant dide do make hys ryche palays that was named
ylion' (p. 508, and so always).   So too Chaucer, *Legend of
Good Women* 936-37:

> In al the noble tour of Ilioun,
> That of the citee was the cheef dungeoun.

Skeat in a note on *Hous of Fame* 158 shows that this was
the general mediæval usage.   That Shakespeare so uses the
form Ilium is absolutely plain.   This *may* be his meaning
in the use of the other spelling, for the sense is open to

to prove that Shakespeare had ever read the book.   H
knows Hero and Leander as types of devoted lovers.

Hiems.—Mids. 2. 1. 109.

> The seasons alter: hoary-headed frosts
> Fall in the fresh lap of the crimson rose,
> And on old Hiems' thin and icy crown
> An odorous chaplet of sweet summer buds
> Is, as in mockery, set.

(The early editions read 'chin and icy crown'; the reading
'thin' is Tyrwhitt's suggestion.)   As has already been
noticed by Malone, this description of Winter is to be traced
to Golding's translation of *Met.* 2. 30:

> Et glacialis Hiems canos hirsuta capillos.

Golding renders, p. 17a and b:

> And lastly quaking for the colde, stood Winter all forlorne,
> With rugged heade as white as Dove, and garments all to torne,
> Forladen with the Icycles that dangled up and downe
> Uppon his gray and hoarie bearde and snowie frozen crowne.

Though Shakespeare has used the Latin form, Hiems, his
lines would seem to have been drawn from Golding's expansion of the single line of the original Latin.   Cf. also LLL
5. 2. 901.

Hesperides.—See Hercules.

Hydra.—See Hercules.

Hymen.—Ado 5. 3. 32; As 5. 4. 114-152; Hml. 3. 2. 169; Tim.
  4. 3. 384; Tp. 4. 1. 23, 97; Per. 3. prol. 9; Tit. 1. 1. 325
  (Hymenæus).

Hymen, the divinity of marriage, was a frequent personage in the masque.   In As 5. 4. he leads in the restored
Rosalind.   As indicated in Tp., he is represented as bearing
a torch.   Cf. *Met.* 4. 758; *Her.* 11. 101, etc.   In Tim.
'Hymen' equals 'marriage.'   Cf. *Met.* 1. 480.

Hyperion.—See Sun-divinities.

reasonable doubt in every instance. It would be difficult to find any authority for a distinction.

Iris.—Alls 1. 3. 158; Troil. 1. 3. 380; Tp. 4. 1; H6B 3. 2. 407.

Iris, originally the rainbow, becomes, from her position between heaven and earth, like Hermes, a messenger of the gods, more especially of Hera. But in the strongly anthropomorphic atmosphere of the Homeric poems her connection with the rainbow is preserved only in epithets such as χρυσόπτερος (*Il.* 8. 398; 11. 185). In Vergil (and in Ovid), on the other hand, the nature-aspect of Iris reasserts itself. Thus in *Æn.* 5. 609 she descends along the many-colored bow ; and in *Æn.* 4. 700-702 :

> Ergo Iris croceis per cælum roscida pinnis
> Mille trahens varios adverso sole colores
> Devolat.

In the masque in Tp. the conception of Iris is strongly Vergilian. She is necessarily a personality distinct from the rainbow, for she appears on the stage ; but she calls herself the 'watery arch and messenger' of Juno, and her connection with the rainbow is further marked in the following lines addressed to her by Ceres :

> Hail, many-colored messenger, that ne'er
> Dost disobey the wife of Jupiter ;
> Who with thy saffron wings upon my flowers
> Diffusest honey-drops, refreshing showers,
> And with each end of thy blue bow dost crown
> My bosky acres.

The first of these lines suggests the 'nuntia Iunonis varios induta colores' of *Met.* 1. 270, while the third and fourth may be referred with some confidence to *Æn.* 4. 700-702 (quoted above). That the Vergilian passage may have been read in Phaer's translation is suggested by the verbal correspondences with Shakespeare in the following line :

Dame Rainbow down therfore with safron wings of dropping shours.

In Alls and Troil. Iris loses all personality, and becomes merely a name for the rainbow. (The meaning of the passage in Alls is made clear by a comparison with Lucr. 1587.) Diametrically opposed to this conception of Iris is that in H6B, where she is thought of merely as a messenger.

Io.—Shr. Ind. 2. 56. See Jupiter.

Ixion (?).—Lr. 4. 7. 47.

Lear says to Cordelia:

> You do me wrong to take me out o' the grave:
> Thou art a soul in bliss; but I am bound
> Upon a wheel of fire, that mine own tears
> Do scald like molten lead.

This suggests the fate of Ixion: *Georg.* 3. 38; *Met.* 4. 460. If one could assume that Shakespeare knew the story of Ixion as contained in Apollodorus 1. 8. 2, the allusion would be especially appropriate, since the theme of the myth, like that of Lr., is ingratitude.

Janus.—Merch. 1. 1. 50; Oth. 1. 2. 33.

In Merch., Salario says:

> Now, by two-headed Janus,
> Nature hath framed strange fellows in her time:
> Some that will evermore peep through their eyes
> And laugh like parrots at a bag-piper,
> And other of such vinegar aspect
> That they'll not show their teeth in way of smile,
> Though Nestor swear the jest be laughable.

On this Eccles comments: 'Because Janus had two countenances, a laughing and a sad.' The phrase 'Iane biceps' occurs in *Fasti* 1. 65. Iago's oath by Janus in Oth. is to be explained either by the fact that Iago is a soldier and Janus is a god of war, or that, as Warburton suggested, 'there is great propriety in making the double Iago swear by Janus, who had two faces.'

Jason.—Merch. 1. 1. 172; 3. 2. 244. See Argonauts.

Jove.—See Jupiter.

Juno.

Juno is unfortunate among the dwellers on Olympus in that she has totally lost her original significance as a nature-myth, and has not, like Minerva, taken on any deep ethical significance. In Vergil and Ovid her actions are almost without exception due to an anger which has its roots in jealousy—not an exalted conception of divinity. Shakespeare mentions Juno 20 times by name and once by implication, but never with any great significance. In Cor. 4. 2. 53; 5. 3. 46 and in Cymb. 3. 4. 168 her anger and jealousy are the points of allusion, and in Alls 3. 4. 13 her anger against Hercules in particular is referred to. In LLL 4. 3. 118 and Wint. 4. 4. 121 she is a type of beauty; while in Tp. 4. 1. 102 and Per. 5. 1. 112 the majesty of her port is mentioned. Thus in Tp., as she is about to enter in the masque, Ceres says:

> Great Juno comes; I know her by her gait.

This is to be traced, directly or indirectly, to the 'divom incedo regina' of *Æn.* 1. 46, though strongly suggesting the 'vera incessu patuit dea' of *Æn.* 1. 405, where the poet is speaking of Venus. From the masque in Tp. we also learn that she is sister to Ceres (both were daughters of Saturn and Rhea), and that she was drawn through the air by peacocks. For this latter conception authority is found in *Met.* 2. 532.

The mention of 'Juno's swans' in As 1. 3. 77 is a famous Shakespearian crux. Venus' swans are mentioned in *Met.* 10. 708, 717, 718, and Shakespeare's slip is the more remarkable because, as Wright has noticed, these lines are included in the story of Venus and Adonis.

In As 1. 3. 77; Tp. 4. 1.; Per. 2. 3. 30, Juno is exercising her common classical function as patroness of marriage.

With one exception, allusions to Juno do not appear earlier than As.

Jupiter.

As principal and supreme divinity, Shakespeare, like
many authors of the Renaissance, identifies Jove with
the Christian God; so that in a play with pagan background, like Cymb. or Wint., the name 'Jove' is used
as the equivalent of 'God.' Even in plays the scenes of
which are laid in Christian times the same substitution is
not uncommon, due in part, perhaps, to the statute against
profanation. This substitution is particularly frequent
in Tw.

Of the attributes of Jove, the thunder is most often mentioned by Shakespeare—an attribute, it will be noticed, which
Jove has in common with the Hebrew Jehovah. He is called
'Thunder-bearer' in Lr. 2. 4. 231, and 'Thunder-darter' in
Troil. 2. 3. 12, while the phrase 'Jupiter tonans' of *Met.* 1.
170, etc., is reproduced in the 'By Jove that thunders' of Ant.
3. 13. 85. At times the conception becomes Hebraic rather
than classical. Thus in H5. 2. 4. 100,

> Therefore in fierce tempest is he coming,
> In thunder and in earthquake, like a Jove,

one is reminded of the voice out of the whirlwind in Job
38. 1, or the voice which came to Elijah in 1 Kings 19. 11, 12.
Again, in Cor. 4. 5. 109,

> If Jupiter
> Should from yond cloud speak divine things,
> And say 'Tis true,'

there seems to be a reminiscence of Matthew 17. 5: 'Behold
a voice out of the cloud, saying, This is my beloved Son . . .;
hear ye him,' In Oth. 2. 1. 77,

> Great Jove, Othello guard,
> And swell his sail with thine own powerful breath,

we have again a Hebraic rather than a classical conception.
Cf. Job 37. 10; Psalm 18. 15. In one instance, Ant. 1. 2.
157, Jove is spoken of as the sender of rain (compare the
phrase, 'Jupiter pluvius').

Other attributes mentioned are the eagle: Cymb. 4. 2. 348;
5. 4. 92 etc., and the oak: As 3. 2. 250; Tp. 5. 1. 45; H6C
5. 2. 14. The eagle is called 'Iovis armiger' in *Æn.* 5. 255;
9. 564, and it is the eagle which carries away Ganymede.
The conception of Jove as descending on the eagle's back
(Cymb. 5. 4. 92) is not classical, suggesting rather a vision
of Ezekiel. The oak as Jove's peculiar tree may be referred
to the 'magna Iovis quercus' of *Georg.* 3. 332, or better to
Met. 1. 106, which Golding translates (p. 5b):

> The acornes dropt on ground from Ioves brode tree in feelde.

Compare with this As 3. 2. 249, which suggests a possible
verbal indebtedness: 'I found him under a tree, like a
dropped acorn. It may well be called *Jove's tree,* when it
drops such fruit.'

In one instance (Troil. 4. 5. 191) Jupiter is spoken of as
'dealing life,' a conception which is reflected in the phrase:
'hominum sator atque deorum' of *Æn.* 1. 254.

The erotic myths connected with Jove receive compara-
tively little attention. This side of Jove's character is alluded
to without specific reference in LLL 4. 3. 117, 144; Oth. 2.
3. 17 (?); Cymb. 5. 4. 33; H6B 4. 1. 47; Per. 1. 1. 7. The
story of Io, related in *Met.* 1. 588-600, is alluded to once, in
Shr. Ind. 2. 56, as the subject of a picture. There is also one
allusion to Ganymede, As 1. 3. 127; see *Met.* 10. 155 seq.
Leda, too, receives one mention, Wiv. 5. 5. 7; see *Her.*
16. 55. A possible allusion to Danae and the shower of gold
is found in Rom. 1. 1. 120; see *Am.* 2. 19. 27-8. The
story of Europa was apparently more familiar: H4B 2. 2.
192; Wiv. 5. 5. 3; Ado 5. 4. 45; Troil. 5. 1. 59; Wint. 4. 4.
27; Shr. 1. 1. 174; it is told at length in *Met.* 2. 846-876.
In Ado there is reference to the 'amiable low' of the metamorphosed Jupiter, which may be referred to l. 851; Golding
translates: 'Goes lowing gently up and downe.' The allusion in Shr. is more detailed:

> O yes, I saw sweet beauty in her face,
> Such as the daughter of Agenor had,
> That made great Jove to humble him to her hand,
> When with his knees he kiss'd the Cretan strand.

6

That Europa is daughter of Agenor is told in l. 858.   In l. 2. of Bk. 3 we are told that the land to which Europa was carried was 'Dictæa rura'; for this Golding substitutes 'Ile of Crete.'   For the idea of his kneeling on the strand I find no definite antecedent.   The allusion to the Europa story in Wint. is taken over bodily from *Dorastus and Fawnia* (Hazlitt's *Shak. Library* Pt. I, Vol. 4, p. 62), from which the plot of Wint. is borrowed.   Under this heading may also be considered Juliet's lines in Rom. 2. 2. 92-93, 'At lovers' perjuries, they say, Jove laughs,' obviously a translation of 'Juppiter ex alto periuria ridet amantum,' *Art.* 1. 633; though Dyce points out that it might have come to Shakespeare from Bojardo's *Orlando Innam.* 1. 22. 42.

Another Ovidian story, that of Jove's entertainment by the humble old couple, Philemon and Baucis, *Met.* 8. 630, is twice referred to: Ado 2. 1. 100; As 3. 3. 11.   In each of these passages Philemon's house is said to be 'thatched.' Golding tells us 'The roofe therof was thatched all with straw and fennish reede' (p. 113b).

Special notice must be given to the masque in Cymb. 5. 4, where 'Jupiter descends in thunder and lightning sitting upon an eagle; he throws a thunderbolt.'   The whole episode is distinctly modern—in certain details Hebraic rather than classical.   'As men report Thou orphans' father art' ll. 39-40 echoes the phrase 'A father of the fatherless,' Psalm 68. 5.   In l. 81 Sicilius prays: 'The crystal window ope; look out,' with which cf. 'The windows of heaven were opened,' Genesis 7. 11.   'Whom best I love I cross,' l. 101, is little more than a paraphrase of Hebrews 12. 6.   The 'marble mansion' of l. 87 means of course the clouds; and is a modern rather than a classical conception.

I am at a loss to explain what is meant by 'Jove's own book,' Cor. 3. 1. 293, unless here, too, we are to look for a Biblical reminiscence.

Laertes.—Tit. 1. 1. 380.

Ulysses is called 'wise Laertes' son.'

Leander.—See Hero.

Leda.—Wiv. 5. 5. 7. See Jupiter. Shr. 1. 2. 244. See Helen.

Lethe.—See Hades.

Lichas.—Merch. 2. 1. 32; Ant. 4. 12. 45. See Hercules.

Love.—See Cupid and Venus.

Lucina.—Cymb. 5. 4. 43; Per. 1. 1. 8; 3. 1. 10.

Lucina is properly an epithet of Juno (or of Diana) as patroness of childbirth, i. e. the one who brings to light. She is mentioned often in Ovid, e. g. *Met.* 9. 294; 10. 510. None of the Shakespearian allusions connect her with either Juno or Diana.

Mars.

Shakespeare's allusions to Mars, though frequent, are for the most part highly conventional. He is either the patron divinity of war, or a type of martial valor and manly strength, but never a mere personification of, or synonym for, war. This conventional use of his name is especially common in the warlike plays, such as the histories, Troil., Ant., and Cor.

There are a few instances of more detailed allusion. Thus in Hml. 2. 2. 512 and Troil. 4. 5. 255 we hear of his armor forged by the hammers of the Cyclopes (in *Æn.* 8. 407-453 they forge him a car and flying wheels), and in five passages allusion is made to his intrigue with Venus: Ven. 98; Troil. 5. 2. 165; Ant. 1. 5. 18; Tp. 4. 1. 98; Tit. 2. 1. 89. The story, first told in *Odys.* 8. 266 seq., is retold by Ovid in *Art.* 2. 561 seq., and more briefly in *Met.* 4. 171 seq.

In Troil. 3. 3. 190 we have, as Steevens has pointed out, an obvious allusion to *Iliad* 5. 864-898, where Mars, wounded by Diomed, is rebuked for his interference in the battle. A further allusion to the incident is found in Cymb. 5. 4. 32; Sicilius says to Jupiter:

> With Mars fall out, with Juno chide
> That thy adulteries
> Rates and revenges.

With this compare *Il.* 5. 889-893 where Jupiter says to Mars (Chapman's translation, p. 81) :

> Thou many minds, inconstant, changeling thou,
> Sit not complaining thus by me, whom most of all the Gods
> Inhabiting the starry hill I hate; no periods
> Being set to thy contentions, brawls, fights and pitching fields;
> Just of thy mother Juno's moods, stiff-necked, and never yields,
> Though I correct her still and *chide*.

The coupling of Mars and Juno, and the word *chide,* seem significant.

Possibly a further indebtedness to *Il.* 5 is to be found in the phrase 'speak as loud as Mars,' Ant. 2. 2. 6. In *Il.* 5. 859-861, when wounded, 'Brazen Ares bellowed loud as nine thousand warriors or ten thousand cry in battle as they join in strife and fray.' It must be remembered, however, that Chapman's translation of *Il.* 5 was not published till 1610, which makes it hard to explain the allusion in Troil. May we assume that Shakespeare might have read this book of Chapman in manuscript?

Mars as a planetary influence is several times referred to.

Medea.—Merch. 5. 1. 13; H6B 5. 2. 59. See Argonauts.

Menelaus.—H6C 2. 2. 147; Troil. passim.

In H6C Menelaus is merely mentioned as Helen's husband. The Menelaus of Troil. is based on Caxton.

Mercury.

Originally a divinity of cloud and storm, Mercury becomes, from his position between heaven and earth, like the rainbow Iris, a messenger of Jove, an instrument by which the gods may carry out their will on earth. It is in this capacity as winged messenger that Shakespeare thinks of him in the majority of instances. Often he is no more than a type of swiftness, or merely a synonym for 'messenger' (cf. Wiv. 2. 2. 82). Two allusions of this sort deserve special attention. In K. J. 4. 2. 174 we read:

> Be Mercury, set feathers to thy heels,
> And fly like thought from them to me again.

With this cf. *Met.* 1. 671-72:

> Parva mora est alas pedibus virgamque potenti
> Somniferam sumpsisse manu tegumenque capillis.

In Golding's version of these lines (p. 14b), 'He made no long abod, but tyde his *fethers* too his feete,' one is tempted to discover a verbal correspondence. In Hml. 3. 4. 58 Hamlet says that his father had

> A station like the herald Mercury
> New-lighted on a heaven-kissing hill,

which strongly suggests the following lines from *Æn.* 4. 246-253:

> Iamque volans apicem et latera ardua cernit
> Atlantis duri, cælum qui vertice fulcit,
> .   .   .   .
> Hic primum paribus nitens Cyllenius alis
> Constitit.

Though the wings of Mercury are so often spoken of, there is but one allusion to his magic wand, in Troil. 2. 3. 13, where mention is made of the 'serpentine craft of his caduceus.' That the wand was wreathed with serpents was a later Latin tradition; Steevens adduces Martial, *Epig.* 7. 74; Marlowe speaks of his 'snaky rod' in *Hero and Leander* 1.

This notion of 'serpentine craft' brings us to the Roman conception of Mercury as the crafty patron of merchants, a conception which naturally grew out of Mercury the messenger. In Tw. 1. 5. 105 Feste says:

> Now Mercury endue thee with leasing.

Cf. *Fasti* 5, where the Roman merchant prays to Mercury to make him clever in lies. So, too, in Wint. 4. 3. 25 the rogue Autolycus was 'littered under Mercury.' To Mercury's gifts in oratory there is an apparent allusion in LLL 5. 2. 940. The allusion to the 'pipe of Hermes' in H5. 3. 7. 19 is to be referred to *Met.* 1. 677 seq., where Mercury charms asleep the monster, Argus, by the music of his pipe.

It is not so easy to explain satisfactorily the following line from Troil. 2. 2. 45:

> And fly like chidden Mercury from Jove.

May it refer to an episode in Marlowe's *Hero and Leander*
1, where Mercury steals nectar from heaven to win the grati-
tude of a shepherd girl, and is severely rebuked therefor by
Jove? For Marlowe's fable, as for Shakespeare's line, I have
found no satisfactory classical antecedent.

Mermaid.—See Sirens.

Merops.—Gent. 3. 1. 153. See Phaeton.

Midas.—Merch. 3. 2. 102.

> Therefore, thou gaudy gold,
> Hard food for Midas.

Midas had the power of turning all that he touched to gold,
see *Met.* 11. 100 seq. (Golding, p. 141a). L. 124 relates
how even his food was transmuted in his mouth, and how
in consequence poor Midas was like to have starved.

Minerva.—Cymb. 5. 5. 164; Shr. 1. 1. 84; H4A 4. 1. 114 (?).

In Cymb. the image of 'straight-pight Minerva' is a type
of beauty. I cannot discover that the epithet corresponds to
any of the recognized epithets of Minerva in Greek or Latin
literature. In Shr. she is mentioned as a type of wisdom.
The 'fire-eyed maid of smoky war' in H4A is probably to be
interpreted as Minerva. Chapman calls her 'war's tri-
umphant maid' in *Il.* 7, and the epithet 'fire-eyed' corresponds to Homer's epithet 'glaukopis.' The name Pallas
does not occur in Shakespeare except in Tit. (4. 1. 66),
though it is common in Elizabethan authors. It is not easy
to explain the paucity of Shakespeare's allusions to Minerva.

Minos, Minotaur.—See Dædalus.

Muse.—Mids. 5. 1. 52; H5. Prol. 1; Oth. 2. 1. 128; and in Sonn.
seventeen times.

Usually the word Muse is merely equivalent to 'poetic
talent.' Twice there is mention of *nine* muses: Mids. 5. 1.
52; Sonn. 38. 9; and in Sonn. 85. 4, 'all the Muses.' In
Sonn. 78. 1 Shakespeare invokes his friend to be his Muse.
The Muses are never mentioned in connection with Apollo.

Music of the Spheres.—Merch. 5. 1. 60; Tw. 3. 1. 121; As 2. 7. 6;
Ant. 5. 2. 84; Per. 5. 1. 231.

Only the first of these passages requires special attention.
Lorenzo says:

> Look how the floor of heaven
> Is thick inlaid with patines of bright gold:
> There's not the smallest orb which thou behold'st
> But in his motion like an angel sings,
> Still quiring to the young-eyed cherubins;
> Such harmony is in immortal souls;
> But whilst this muddy vesture of decay
> Doth grossly close it in, we cannot hear it.

Elze thinks Shakespeare took this from Montaigne's essay
On Custom. As Florio's translation did not appear till
1603, he would have had to read it in the French. I fail to
find in the passage any sufficient reason for thinking Shakespeare had seen it. In a note on Tw. 3. 1. 121, Furness
refers us to Plato, *Republic* 10. 14. This is, of course, the
ultimate source; but Furness does not suggest how it
reached Shakespeare. Shakespeare may have met the idea
in Cicero's *Somnium Scipionis.* The passage closes with
these words: 'Now this sound, which is effected by the rapid
rotation of the whole system of nature, is so powerful, that
human hearing cannot comprehend it; just as you cannot
look directly upon the sun, because your sight and sense are
overcome by his beams' (trans. Edmonds). However, the
idea is a common one for which it is rash to assign a definite
source.

Myrmidons.—Tw. 2. 3. 29. See Achilles.

Naiads.—Tp. 4. 1. 128.

In the masque of Act 4 Iris summons up the Naiads,
describing them as 'nymphs of the windring brooks.' In
Tp. 1. 2. 316 Ariel enters like a water-nymph.

Narcissus.—Ven. 161; Lucr. 265; Ant. 2. 5. 96.

In Ant. Narcissus is referred to merely as a type of irre-

sistible beauty.　The first two citations allude to his fatal
love for his own image.　In Ven.:

> Narcissus so himself himself forsook
> And died to kiss his shadow in the brook.

In Lucr.:

> That had Narcissus seen her as she stood,
> Self-love had never drown'd him in the flood.

Comparing these allusions with the account in *Met.* 3. 407
seq., we notice that Shakespeare does not mention the metamorphosis into a flower, but thinks of Narcissus as drowned
in the water on which he gazed.　That this more prosaic
version of the story was not unknown to the ancients is
shown by Eustathius, *Comm. ad Homeri Iliadem,* p. 266, line
7.　That it was not unfamiliar to the Elizabethans may be
shown from Marlowe's *Hero and Leander* 1. 74.　I am
inclined to believe, however, that Shakespeare's immediate
source may have been a poem of 264 lines in Latin hexa-
meters by one John Clapham, entitled *Narcissus, sive Amoris
Juvenilis et Præcipue Philautiæ Brevis atque Moralis De-
scriptio*, published by Thomas Scarlet, London, 1591, a copy
of which is preserved in the British Museum.　The closing
lines of this poem are as follows:

> Hæc ubi dicta dedit tendens ad sidera palmas,
> Terque gemens dicit pereo, formose valeto,
> Dure nimis, repetens iterum, formosè valeto.
> Deficiunt vires, et vox et spiritus ipse
> Deficit, et pronus de ripa decidit, et sic
> Ipse suæ periit deceptus imaginis umbra.

We have here the death by drowning, and in the title of
the composition the 'self-love' of Shakespeare's lines.

Not to push the similarity between the 'periit deceptus
imaginis umbra' and the last line quoted from Ven., one may
notice that the only detailed allusions to Narcissus in Shakespeare occur in poems published in 1594 and 1593 respectively, or within four years of the date of Clapham's *Narcis-*

sus, and that Clapham's poem is, like the two poems of Shakespeare, dedicated to Henry, Earl of Southampton.

Nature.

Shakespeare's Nature is merely a personification of a philosophical abstraction, properly not mythological at all. I shall merely enumerate the more significant aspects which the personification takes. Any attempt to trace the ultimate sources of the conception would take us far afield in ancient and mediæval philosophy.

She is the power which gives to the created universe its form. Thus she is spoken of as 'molding' (Cymb. 5. 4. 48) or 'framing' (Ven. 744; Merch. 1. 1. 51), and once as 'forging Nature' (Ven. 729). It is she who frames the human body, determining its physical appearance (Ado 3. 1. 63; Mids. 5. 1. 416; Ven. 744); thus she has to do with childbirth (Wint. 2. 2. 60; Lr. 1. 4. 297). Not only the physical but moral stature of man is of her forging (Ado 3. 1. 49; Meas. 1. 1. 37; Cymb. 4. 2. 170). Still more interesting is the conception of her in H4B 1. 1. 153 as the spirit of order which keeps the world from relapsing into chaos:

> Let heaven kiss earth! Now let not Nature's hand
> Keep the wild flood confined! let order die.

Somewhat similar are the curses in Lr. 3. 2. 8 and Wint. 4. 4. 488; cf. also Mcb. 4. 1. 59.

In this function of fashioner and preserver she encounters several powers more or less hostile. As 'sovereign mistress over wrack' she is opposed in Sonn. 126. 5 to the destroyer, Time. In Ven. 733 the Destinies cross her 'curious workmanship.' Fortune is opposed to her in Wiv. 3. 3. 69, and that the opposition is frequent is implied by K. J. 3. 1. 52. She is contrasted with art in Wint. 4. 4. 83 ff.; 5. 2. 108.

Deserving of special attention are the Friar's words in Rom. 2. 3. 9:

> The earth that's nature's mother is her tomb;
> What is her burying grave, that is her womb,

which Steevens would refer to Lucretius 5. 260:

> Omniparens eadem rerum commune sepulchrum.

Nectar.—Ven. 572; Gent. 2. 4. 171; Troil. 3. 2. 23.

Nectar is mentioned only three times, and never with definite mythological allusion. Ambrosia is never mentioned.

Nemean Lion.—See Hercules.

Nemesis.—H6A 4. 7. 78.

Talbot is called the 'terror and black Nemesis' of France. The word is used loosely as about equivalent to 'agent of destruction.' The divinity is not mentioned by either Ovid or Vergil; she is, however, the subject of one of Whitney's Emblems, p. 19.

Neptune.

Shakespeare's treatment of Neptune is rather colorless. His chariot is nowhere mentioned; his trident is referred to but twice, Cor. 3. 1. 256; Tp. 1. 2. 204. In other words, he is not a divinity but a personification, more or less vivid, of the sea. In Mids. 3. 2. 392; Tp. 5. 1. 35; Wint. 5. 1. 154; Per. 3. 3. 36, the personal element is nearly, if not quite, absent, as shown by the definite article in *'the* ebbing Neptune,' *'the* dreadful Neptune.' (Troil. 1. 3. 45 should probably be included here: a wrecked ship is spoken of as a toast for Neptune, where the ship is apparently compared to a piece of toast soaked in a cup, of wine (cf. Wiv. 3. 5. 3) or soup). In R2. 2. 1. 63; Ant. 4. 14. 58; Cymb. 3. 1. 19 there is a half-personification, while in K. J. 5. 2. 34; Troil. 5. 2. 174; Ant. 2. 7. 139; Tim. 5. 4. 78, Neptune is accredited with eyes, ears, and arms. Perhaps the most vivid personification is in H4B 3. 1. 51:

> and, other times, to see
> The beachy girdle of the ocean
> Too wide for Neptune's hips.

In a few instances, Mids. 2. 1. 127; Hml. 1. 1. 119; 3. 2. 166; Mcb. 2. 2. 60; Per. 3. prol. 45, Neptune is spoken of as *owning* the sea, in such phrases as: 'Neptune's yellow sands' (Mids.), 'Neptune's ocean' (Mcb.), 'Neptune's empire,' (Hml. 1). In Per. 3. 1. 1. he is 'god of this great vast,' and his worship is alluded to in 5. prol. 17 and 5. 1. 17.

There is but one allusion to the mythology of Neptune in the narrower sense, i. e. his metamorphosis into a ram in order to seduce Theophane (*Met.* 6. 117), but this allusion, Wint. 4. 4. 28, is borrowed bodily from *Dorastus and Fawnia,* the main source of Wint. See Hazlitt's *Shak. Libr.* Pt. I, Vol. 4, p. 62.

Nereides.—Ant. 2. 2. 211.

The Nereides are referred to but once, in a description of Cleopatra's barge, where the word is taken over from the description in North's Plutarch, *Life of Antonius* (Temple ed. p. 34). 'Her ladies and gentlewomen also, the fairest of them were apparelled like the nymphs Nereids (which are the mermaids of the waters) and like the Graces, some steering the helm, others tending the tackle and ropes of the barge, etc.'

Nessus.—Alls 4. 3. 281; Ant. 4. 12. 43; As 2. 3. 14-15 (?). See Hercules.

Nestor.—LLL 4. 3. 169; Lucr. 1401 ff.; Merch. 1. 1. 56; H6A 2. 5. 6; H6C 3. 2. 188.

The allusions to Nestor outside of Troil., where he appears as one of the *dramatis personæ,* are all earlier than 1596. He is in every instance a type of age, dignity, or wise counsel and oratory. In Troil., also, the characterization of Nestor does not go much beyond these simple traits. He is 'venerable Nestor, hatched in silver,' 1. 3. 65; he was a man 'when Hector's grandsire sucked,' 1. 3. 291. The character is throughout consistent with Homer's Nestor, and there is every reason to believe that Shakespeare had Chapman before him when he wrote Troil. Still, the eloquence and age of

Nestor are mentioned in *Met.* 13. 63-66, and in its broad features the character must have been familiar to Shakespeare from conversation and general reading.

Night.

In four passages, covering the whole range of his activity, Shakespeare speaks of Night as drawn through the sky by a yoke of dragons: Mids. 3. 2. 379; Troil. 5. 8. 17 (the authenticity of the scene has been doubted) ; Cymb. 2. 2. 48; H6B 4. 1. 4.   For such a conception there is no classical authority.   In Ovid, Night is drawn by horses: 'Lente currite noctis equi,' *Am.* 1. 13. 40; 'Sive pruinosi noctis aguntur equi,' *Pont.* 1. 2. 56.   Where did Shakespeare get the idea? I have shown in the article on Hecate that Shakespeare and his contemporaries think of Hecate as driving a dragon-yoke, and in the same article have given my reasons for believing that Shakespeare identifies Hecate with Night.   The dragon-yoke of night, then, is the dragon-yoke of Hecate.

In H5. 4. 1. 288 Shakespeare speaks of 'Horrid night, the child of hell.'   Vergil calls Hades the 'world of shades, of sleep, and slumberous Night,' *Æn.* 6. 390; and in *Fasti* 6. 140 occurs the phrase 'horrenda nocte.'   In Hesiod, *Theog.* 123, Night is a daughter of Chaos and Erebus.

Niobe.—Hml. 1. 2. 149; Troil. 5. 10. 19.

Merely mentioned as a type of excessive weeping.   Ovid tells the story in *Met.* 6. 146-312.   The authenticity of the closing scenes of Troil. has been doubted.

Olympus.—Hml. 5. 1. 277; Cæs. 3. 1. 74;   4. 3. 92;   Oth. 2. 1. 190; Cor. 5. 3. 30;   Tit. 2. 1. 1.

Save in Tit., Olympus is not thought of as the dwelling-place of the gods, but simply as a type of a high and large mountain.   In Hml. 5. 1. 277 Pelion is so mentioned in connection with Olympus, and in Hml. 5. 1. 306 Ossa is similarly referred to.   The three mountains are mentioned together in *Met.* 1. 154-155, in the account of the war of the giants. In ll. 155-6 Ovid says that many of the giants were buried

under Pelion when Jove struck it from the top of Ossa. To
this we may refer Mrs. Page's remark in Wiv. 2. 1. 81, 'I
had rather be a giantess and lie under Mount Pelion.'

Orpheus.—Mids. 5. 1. 49; Gent. 3. 2. 78; Lucr. 553; Merch. 5. 1.
80; Tit. 2. 4. 51; H8. 3. 1. 3.

The myth of Orpheus represents to Shakespeare, as to the
ancients, the power of music and poetry as a civilizing and
pacifying force. In his earliest and in his latest plays he
recognizes the soothing power of music. Thus in Mids.
2. 1. 150-152:

> (I) heard a mermaid on a dolphin's back
> Uttering such dulcet and harmonious breath
> That the rude sea grew civil at her song;

and in Tp. 1. 2. 391-92 Ferdinand says:

> This music crept by me upon the waters,
> Allaying both their fury and my passion;

and 'soft music' play its part in restoring harmony to the
'untuned and jarring senses' of the 'child-changed' Lear.

In Merch. 5. 1, after describing the soothing effect of
music on a herd of young colts, Lorenzo says:

> Therefore the poet
> Did feign that Orpheus drew trees, stones, and floods;
> Since nought so stockish, hard, and full of rage,
> But music for the time doth change his nature.

The poet referred to is probably Ovid, who tells the story
of Orpheus in *Met.* 10 and 11. At the beginning of Book
11 we read:

> Carmine dum tali silvas animosque ferarum
> Threicius vates et saxa sequentia ducit.

(It is possibly worth noting that Golding translates *ducit*
in this line by *draws*.) Neither Ovid nor Vergil says that
Orpheus drew floods; but in Horace, *Od.* 1. 12. 7-10:

> Unde vocalem temere insecutæ
>   Orphea silvæ.
> Arte materna rapidos morantem
> Fluminum lapsus celeresque ventos.

Compare also Medea's incantation in *Met.* 7. 197-206.

In Gent. 3. 2. Proteus advises Thurio to win his lady's heart by writing poems to her:

> For Orpheus' lute was strung with poets' sinews,
> Whose golden touch could soften steel and stones,
> Make tigers tame and huge leviathans
> Forsake unsounded deeps to dance on sands.

For the idea expressed in the first line I find no classical authority. Eratosthenes, *Catasterismi* 24, says that Mercury made Orpheus' lyre out of a tortoise shell and the sinews of the cattle of Apollo; but of course Shakespeare did not know the obscure mythographer. Warburton has an over-subtle note in which he declares that Shakespeare is alluding to the legislative power of Orpheus. It may mean only that the music of the lute depends on the words of the poet for its effectiveness; the context would bear out this interpretation. The second line is explained by *Met.* 11. 7-12: until the Thracian women drowned his music with their cries, javelins and stones fell harmless at his feet. The taming of tigers is mentioned by Vergil, *Georg.* 4. 510. It is at least a curious coincidence that Vergil puts the story into the mouth of Proteus, the sea-divinity, while the Shakespearian lines are spoken by the Veronese gentleman, his namesake (cf. s. v. Proteus). For the last line I find no authority. Further from the Latin originals is the charming song of Queen Katherine in H8. 3. 1. The reference to Orpheus' death in Mids. 5. 1. 49 suggests the possibility of a contemporary play on the subject; but of this I find no trace.

Orpheus' descent into Hades is mentioned rather inappropriately in Lucr. 553:

> And moody Pluto winks while Orpheus plays.

This may have been suggested by *Met.* 10. 40-44 or *Georg.* 4. 481-484, though not definitely stated in either passage. The 'tenuitque inhians tria Cerberus ora' of the second passage probably suggested Tit. 2. 4. 51. In *Æn.* 6. 417-425, where Cerberus disputes the passage of Æneas, the Sibyl puts him asleep with a drugged cake. Shakespeare may have confused this with the story of Orpheus.

It will be noticed that all the allusions to Orpheus in the genuine plays come between 1590 and 1596. On 26 Aug. 1595 was entered on the Stat. Reg. a poem called 'Orpheus, his Journey to Hell,' falsely attributed to Richard Barnfield.

Ossa.—Hml. 5. 1. 306. See Olympus.

Pallas.—Tit. 4. 1. 66. See Minerva.

Pandar(us).—See Troilus.

Paris.—Lucr. 1473; H6A 5. 5. 104; Shr. 1. 2. 247; Troil. passim.

In Lucr. the lust of Paris is mentioned as occasioning the fall of Troy. In Shr. he is a type of the successful suitor. In H6A his journey to Greece to get Helen is mentioned. For such indefinite allusion to a common story, no specific source is to be assigned. His character and action in Troil. is derived from Caxton. One passage alone deserves particular attention. In 2. 2. 110 Cassandra says:

> Our firebrand brother, Paris, burns us all,

alluding to the fact that Hecuba, when big with Paris, dreamed she was delivered of a firebrand, *Her.* 16. 45-46. This fact is not mentioned by Caxton. Cf. s. v. Althæa.

Pegasus.—See Perseus.

Pelion.—Wiv. 2. 1. 81; Hml. 5. 1. 277. See Olympus.

Penelope.—Cor. 1. 3. 92. See Ulysses.

Penthesilea.—Tw. 2. 3. 193.

Sir Toby playfully calls Maria Penthesilea. Penthesilea was queen of the Amazons. Her name is mentioned by

Ovid in *Art.* 3. 2; *Her.* 21. 118.   She also appears in Caxton, as Pantesilee.

Perigenia.—Mids. 2. 1. 78.   See Theseus.

Perseus.

Shakespeare's acquaintance with Perseus is not great.   He is mentioned by name three times (H5. 3. 7. 22; Troil. 1. 3. 42; 4. 5. 186) as a horseman, and the first passage shows that he is thought of as riding Pegasus (see H5. 3. 7. 15). The only connection between Perseus and Pegasus recognized by the ancients is that, as Ovid relates, *Met.* 4. 785, Pegasus sprang from the blood of Medusa when Perseus cut off her head.   Troil. 1. 3. 42 would indicate that Shakespeare, like Spenser (*Ruins of Time* 649), thinks of Perseus as mounted on Pegasus in his struggle with the sea-monster at the rescue of Andromeda.   In the Ovidian account, *Met.* 4. 663 seq., he is represented as flying out over the sea on winged sandals.   It is easy to see how the confusion occurred, since Perseus rescued Andromeda soon after his encounter with Medusa.   (It may be worth while to notice that in Rubens' painting of Perseus and Andromeda in the Royal Museum at Berlin, a winged horse stands at the left of the picture.)

In view of these passages it is safe to conclude that in H4A 4. 1. 109 it is to Perseus that Vernon compares Prince Hal:

> As if an angel dropped down from the clouds,
> To turn and wind a fiery Pegasus,
> And witch the world with noble horsemanship.

Compare Jonson, *Underwoods* 71.

Shakespeare thinks of Pegasus as winged, and with fiery nostrils (H5. 3. 7. 15).   The first of these attributes is mentioned by Ovid, *Met.* 5. 256, and Horace, *Od.* 4. 11. 26.   For the second there is no classical authority, though the steeds of the sun breathe fire from their nostrils, *Met.* 2. 84.   Shakespeare never speaks of Pegasus as connected with poetry. Cymb. 3. 2. 50 is an allusion to Pegasus.

The Gorgon is mentioned twice (Mcb. 2. 3. 77; Ant. 2. 5. 116), but not in connection with Perseus, in each case merely as a terrible sight.   As related in *Met.* 5. 189-210; 4. 779-781, the Gorgon's head had the power of turning the spectator to stone.   In Mcb. 2. 3, at the discovery of Duncan's murder, Macduff says:

> Approach the chamber, and destroy your sight
> With a new Gorgon.

Phaeton.—Gent. 3. 1. 153; Rom. 3. 2. 3; R2. 3. 3. 178; H6C 1. 4. 33; 2. 6. 12.

Ovid tells in *Met.* 1. 748—2. 238 how Phaeton, wrongly accused of being the son, not of Phœbus but of the mortal Merops, asked his father Phœbus to let him drive for a day the chariot of the sun, that he might thereby prove his divine parentage.   Phœbus unwillingly consented; but the 'unruly jades' ran away; the heavens and earth were scorched; and the presumptuous driver fell into the river Eridanus. Shakespeare may well have drawn his knowledge of the myth from Ovid, though, save that Golding (p. 22a) calls Phaeton a 'wagoner' (cf. Rom. 3. 2. 2), there are no striking verbal similarities.   As a parallel to Rom.,

> Gallop apace, you fiery-footed steeds,
> Towards Phœbus' lodging: such a waggoner
> As Phaeton would whip you to the west,
> And bring in cloudy night immediately,

Malone quotes the following from Barnabe Riche's *Farewell* (1583): 'The day to his seeming passed away so slowly that he had thought the stately steedes had bin tired that drawe the chariot of the Sunne, and wished that Phaeton had been there with a whip.'

Philomel and Tereus.

In Tit. there are five references to the story of Philomel and Tereus.   Lavinia's fate is compared to that of Philomel; like her she is ravished, and like her deprived of her tongue that the secret may not be told.   Philomel weaves her story

7

into a web, which is sent to her sister Progne; Lavinia, who has lost hands as well as tongue, is yet able to turn over the pages of Ovid's *Metamorphoses* until she comes to the story of her prototype (Tit. 4. 1. 42). The revenge wreaked on Tamora is confessedly suggested by that which Progne devises for Tereus (Tit. 5. 2. 195; cf. *Met*. 6. 646). If we were sure that Shakespeare wrote Tit., the explicit indebtedness to *Met*. 6. 412-676 would make us confident in asserting that Ovid is the book referred to in Cymb. 2. 2. 45:

> She hath been reading late
> The tale of Tereus; here the leaf's turn'd down
> Where Philomel gave up.

Malone notices that the story is the second tale in *A Petite Palace of Pettie his Pleasure* (1576) and that it is also told in Gower's *Conf. Am.* 5. I discover no immediate indebtedness to Gower.

As Philomel was turned into a nightingale, so we have in Mids. 2. 2. 13, and often elsewhere, the name used as equivalent to 'nightingale.' More explicit is the reference in Lucr. 1128 ff., where in l. 1134 Tereus is named.

Phœbe.—See Diana.

Phœbus.—See Sun-divinities.

Phœnix.—As 4. 3. 17; Alls 1. 1. 182; Sonn. 19. 4; Ant. 3. 2. 12; Tim. 2. 1. 32; Tp. 3. 3. 23; Cymb. 1. 6. 17; H6A 4. 7. 93; H6C 1. 4. 35; H8. 5. 5. 41; Lov. Comp. 93; Phœn. and Turtle, passim.

The familiar story of the Phœnix is found in *Met*. 15. 391-407; but for an idea so common in Elizabethan literature one cannot assign a definite source.

Pigmies.—Ado 2. 1. 278; Lr. 4. 6. 171.

Shakespeare's treatment of the Pigmies is not classical. They are mentioned by Homer in *Il*. 3. 6, and described by Pliny in *N. H.* 7. 2; but Shakespeare's mention of them in connection with Prester John and the great Cham suggests rather such an author as Mandeville. Furness quotes Batman *upon Bartholome.*

Pluto.—Lucr. 553; H4B 2. 4. 169; Troil. 4. 4. 129; 5. 2. 102; 5. 2. 153; Cor. 1. 4. 36; Tit. 4. 3. 13; 4. 3. 37.

Pluto is spoken of in each case as god of the lower world, but without any elaboration of allusion. The name Pluto occurs only once in Vergil, *Æn.* 7. 327, and in Ovid not at all. The name Dis, by which Ovid and Vergil designate the deity, is found in Shakespeare only twice, in each case in connection with the rape of Proserpina (q. v.). The name Pluto occurs three times in Seneca. The phrase 'dusky Dis' of Tp. 4. 1. 89 is paralleled by 'Duskie Pluto' in Golding, p. 59a.

Plutus.—Alls 5. 3. 101; Cæs. 4. 3. 102; Troil. 3. 3. 197; 1. 1. 287.

Plutus is, according to the passage in Tim., 'the god of gold'; in Cæs., 'dearer than Plutus' mine' is equivalent to 'more precious than a gold mine.' In Alls he knows the secret of alchemy. He is not mentioned either by Ovid or Vergil. It has been noticed that in the passages cited from Cæs. and Troil. the First Folio reads Pluto instead of Plutus. For a discussion of this fact see *Notes and Queries,* Ser. 9, Vol. 4, p. 265. The name is rightly printed in Alls and Tim.

Priam (and Fall of Troy).—Lucr. 1448, 1466, 1485, 1490; H4B 1. 1. 72; Alls 1. 3. 77; Hml. 2. 2. 469-541; Tit. 1. 1. 80; 3. 1. 69; 5. 3. 80; H6B 1. 4. 20; H6C 2. 5. 120; Shr. 3. 1. 29 ff.

Lucrece sees the death of Priam at the hands of Pyrrhus among the flames of the city depicted in her Troy-picture. The speech of the player in Hml., however, gives a much more detailed account. The Shakespearian authorship of the passage is, of course, open to serious question; the following theories have been advanced: that it is (1) a quotation from a lost play of Shakespeare; (2) an invention of Shakespeare for this occasion; (3) a burlesque of some particular play, e. g. Marlowe's *Dido, Queen of Carthage;* (4) an excerpt from some play now lost. Some editors assert that Hamlet (and Shakespeare) really admires it;

others that it is introduced for satire.   As far as the mythology of the speech goes, there is no reason why Shakespeare might not have written it.   It is based on *Æn.* 2. 438-558, and the source is used with a freedom thoroughly characteristic of Shakespeare.   The speech contains the following information: Pyrrhus leaves the wooden horse and seeks Priam.   Priam has armed himself, and is attacking the Greeks with feeble sword.   Pyrrhus strikes at him, and the mere whiff and wind of his sword overthrows the old king. At this moment flaming Ilium falls with hideous crash. Pyrrhus strikes again, and kills him.   Hecuba, bare-foot and half clad, runs up and down in fear, and at sight of murdered Priam bursts into clamor.   In Vergil we are told that Pyrrhus (Neoptolemus) was one of those concealed in the horse (1. 263).   He attacks the palace in 1. 469 (Vergil speaks of the brassy gleam of his armor, while Shakespeare arms him in black).   Priam arms himself at 1. 509:

> Arma diu senior desueta trementibus ævo
> Circumdat necquicquam humeris, et inutile ferrum
> Cingitur, ac densos fertur moriturus in hostes.

In 1. 465 is described the fall of one of the towers of the palace:

> Ea lapsa repente ruinam
> Cum sonitu trahit, et Danaum super agmina late
> Incidit.

Shakespeare utilizes this touch in the lines:

> Then senseless Ilium,
> Seeming to feel this blow, with flaming top
> Stoops to his base, and with a hideous crash
> Takes prisoner Pyrrhus' ear,

dramatically transposing the order of events to make it coincident with the fall of Priam.   (Shakespeare uses the name Ilium as a designation of Priam's palace, see Ilium.) Priam's death is transacted at 1. 554.   Hecuba is present during the scene, but her scanty clothing is a touch of realism added by Shakespeare in characteristic manner.

That Shakespeare was familiar with *Æn.* 2 is proved by his treatment of Sinon (q. v.) and by a simile in H4B:

> Even such a man, so faint, so spiritless,
> So dull, so dead in look, so woe-begone,
> Drew Priam's curtain in the dead of night,
> And would have told him half his Troy was burnt;
> But Priam found the fire ere he his tongue.

This would seem to be an inaccurate recollection or an intentional adaptation of *Æn.* 2. 268-297, where in a vision of the night 'mæstissimus Hector' appears weeping to Æneas, and warns him of his danger; Æneas awakes to find Troy in flames.

The remaining allusions offer nothing of interest. In Tit. 1 the number of his sons is mentioned; in Shr. his name occurs in a quotation from *Her.* 1. 33-34. The Priam of Troil. is only a minor personage, and his character is not developed. The few details of his action are drawn from Caxton.

Priapus.—Per. 4. 6. 4.

A type of lust. Cf. the story of Lotis in *Fasti* 1. 415 seq., or the similar story in *Fasti* 6. 319 seq.

Procris.—Mids. 5. 1. 201, 202. See Cephalus.

Progne.—Tit. 5. 2. 196. See Philomel.

Prometheus.—LLL 4. 3. 304, 351; Oth. 5. 2. 12; Tit. 2. 1. 17.

Only in Tit. is Prometheus mentioned as the sufferer of Caucasus. To Shakespeare he is rather the fashioner of the human race, as Ovid represents him in *Met.* 1. 82; (but cf. s. v. Tityus.)

As Othello sees the candle burning by Desdemona's bed, he says:

> Put out the light, and then put out the light:
> If I quench thee, thou flaming minister,
> I can again thy former light restore,
> Should I repent me: but once put out thy light,
> Thou cunning'st pattern of excelling nature,
> I know not where is that Promethean heat
> That can thy light relume.

And so in LLL we have an allusion to 'Promethean fire.'
But Ovid mentions only earth and water as the ingredients
of man.   It is not strange, however, that this myth should
have been confused with his theft of fire.   In the Scholia
to Horace. Lib. 1, Od. 3 we find, 'Cum ignis e cœlo furtim
a Prometheo surreptus esset ad suas e terra fictas statuas
animandas.'   Cf. also Fulgentius, *Mythologicon* 2. 9.   The
idea may have reached Shakespeare through Spenser, *F. Q.*
2, 10. 70 :

> It told how first Prometheus did create
> A man, of many parts from beasts deryv'd,
> And then stole fire from heven to animate
> His worke.

With the passage in LLL compare

> Thy favours, like Promethean sacred fire
> In dead and dull conceit can life inspire;

Marston, *Pygmalion's Image* (1598) Dedication, ll. 7. 8;
and,

> In whose bright lookes sparkles the radiant fire,
> Wilie Prometheus slilie stole from Jove,
> Infusing breath, life, motion, soule,
> To everie object striken, by thine eies.

The Taming of a Shrew, Shak. Lib. Pt. II, Vol. 2, p. 510.

Proserpina.—Troil. 2. 1. 37; Tp. 4. 1. 89; Wint. 4. 4. 116.

In the first passage Thersites says : 'Thou art as full of
envy at his greatness as Cerberus is at Proserpina's beauty.'
For this I have found no specific antecedent.   The two
remaining passages refer to the rape of Proserpina by Dis.
In the first Ceres says : 'Since they (i. e. Venus and Cupid)
did plot The means that dusky Dis my daughter got.'   In
Wint., Perdita says :

> O Proserpina,
> For the flowers now, that frighted thou let'st fall
> From Dis's waggon! daffodils,
> That come before the swallow dares, and take
> The winds of March with beauty.

She goes on to enumerate 'violets dim,' 'pale primroses,' 'bold oxlips and the crown imperial,' 'lilies of all kinds, the flower-de-luce being one.' Ovid tells the story in *Met.* 5. 359-550. The plotting of Venus and Cupid is described in l. 363 seq. (The Latin has 'Erycina,' but Golding substitutes 'Venus.') The dropping of the flowers is given in ll. 389-99. As to the flowers themselves, we read in l. 392, 'aut violas aut candida lilia carpit.' In *Fasti* 4. 437-443 a longer list is given:

> Illa legit calthas, huic sunt violaria curæ,
> Illa papavereas subsecat ungue comas:
> Has, hyacinthe, tenes; illas, amarante, moraris;
> Pars thyma, pars casiam, pars meliloton amant.
> Plurima lecta rosa est; sunt et sine nomine flores.
> Ipsa crocos tenues liliaque alba legit.

Proteus.—H6C 3. 2. 192.

> I can add colors to the chameleon,
> Change shapes with Proteus for advantages.

With this compare Golding's expansion of the 'Proteaque ambiguum' of *Met.* 2. 9 (p. 17a):

> Unstable Protew chaunging aye his figure and his hue
> From shape to shape a thousande sithes as list him to renue.

A more detailed account is found in *Georg.* 4. 388 seq., itself a copy of *Odyssey* 4. 384 seq.

It has been suggested that the fickle Proteus in Gent. is named with reference to the changeable water-divinity. Compare what is said of him in the article on Orpheus.

Pygmalion.—Meas. 3. 2. 47.

Lucio asks Pompey: 'What, is there none of Pygmalion's images, newly made woman?' which probably means, as Malone puts it: 'Is there no courtesan, who being *newly made woman,* i. e. *lately debauched,* still retains the appearance of chastity, and looks as cold as a statue?' Shakespeare may have learned the story from *Met.* 10. 243-297; but in 1598 had been published *The Metamorphosis of Pygmalion's*

Image by John Marston.   It is perhaps worth while to quote
a sentence from the 'Argument': 'whereupon Venus, graci-
ously condescending to his earnest suit, the maid (by the
power of her deity) was metamorphosed into a living
woman.'

Pyramus and Thisbe.—Mids. passim; Rom. 2. 4. 45; Merch. 5. 1.
  7; Tit. 2. 3. 231.

The story of Pyramus and Thisbe is told in *Met.* 4. 55-
166, in Chaucer's *Legend of Good Women* 706-923, and in
other less artistic English versions, which Shakespeare may
well have known.   There had even been a brief play on the
subject (see Preface to Temple ed., p. xi).   It is impossible to say with any certainty whence Shakespeare drew
his knowledge of the story.   I have been unable to discover
any verbal correspondences between Mids. and either Ovid
or Chaucer.   The allusion in Merch., however, seems to
suggest Golding:

> In such a night (i. e. moonlight)
> Did Thisbe fearfully o'ertrip the dew,
> And saw the lion's shadow ere himself,
> And ran dismay'd away.

Golding says (p. 52b):

> Whome (i. e. the lioness) Thisbe spying furst
> A farre by moonelight, thereupon with fearfull steppes gan flie.

In Rom. Thisbe is a type of beauty.   In Tit. the allusion
is to the death of Pyramus, and corresponds, though not
verbally, with the Ovidian account.

Pyrrhus.—Lucr. 1467; Hml. 2. 2. 472 ff.; Troil. 3. 3. 209.

For the first two references see Priam.   In Troil. he
is mentioned as 'young Pyrrhus,' son of Achilles, now at
home in Greece.   Cf. Caxton, p. 643.

Rhesus.—H6C 4. 2. 20.   See Ulysses.

Rumor.—See Fame.

Saturn.—H4B 2. 4. 286; Ado 1. 3. 12; Sonn. 98. 4; Cymb. 2. 5. 12; Tit. 2. 3. 31.

Saturn is never in Shakespeare identified with the Greek Kronos as time, or represented as father of the gods. He is the 'melancholy god' referred to in Tw. 2. 4. 75, the cold, melancholy influence which makes men of a phlegmatic or 'Saturnine' humor. Hence he is a planetary and astrological quantity rather than a mythological personage.

Satyrs.—Hml. 1. 2. 140; Wint. 4. 4. 334, 352.

The Satyrs play an unimportant part in Shakespeare's mythology. In Hml. a satyr is mentioned as a type of physical ugliness. In Wint. there is a dance of Satyrs, or as the ignorant servant says, 'they have made themselves all men of hair, they call themselves Saltiers.'

Scylla and Charybdis.—Merch. 3. 5. 19.

Launce says: 'Thus when I shun Scylla, your father, I fall into Charybdis, your mother.' Scylla and Charybdis are described in *Æn.* 3. 420-432, and in *Met.* 13. 730-734, but the word 'shun' would show that Malone is right in referring the passage to the proverb 'Incidis in Scyllam, cupiens vitare Charybdim,' which he assigns to Philippe Gualtier, *Alexandreis* 5.

Semiramis.—Tit. 2. 1. 22; 2. 3. 118; Shr. Ind. 2. 41.

In Tit. Semiramis is merely a type of lust. In Shr. the lord says to Sly:

> Or wilt thou sleep? we'll have thee to a couch
> Softer and sweeter than the lustful bed
> On purpose trimm'd up for Semiramis.

Semiramis, the legendary founder of Babylon, is only alluded to by Ovid. A long account of her wars and of the magnificent gardens she built is given by Diodorus Siculus 2. 1-20; but I am unable to find any reference to the 'lustful bed,' though her lascivious character is sufficiently indicated.

Sibyl.—Merch. 1. 2. 116; Oth. 3. 4. 70; Tit. 4. 1. 105; H6A 1. 2. 56; Shr. 1. 2. 70.

The two allusions in the authentic plays lay stress on the Sibyl's age. Portia says in Merch.: 'If I live to be old as Sibylla'; and in Oth.:

> A sibyl, that had number'd in the world
> The sun to course two hundred compasses,
> In her prophetic fury sew'd the work.

The Cumæan Sibyl in *Met.* 14. 130-154 has lived 'sæcula septem' and has still three hundred years to live; the age of the Sibyl is alluded to also in *Fasti* 3. 534; 4. 875. She is shown in 'prophetic fury' in *Æn.* 6. 45 seq. and 77 seq. Her age is also the point of allusion in Shr. In Tit.—

> The angry northern wind
> Will blow these sands, like Sibyl's leaves, abroad—

we have a reminiscence of *Æn.* 6. 74-76, where Æneas prays the Sibyl:

> Foliis tantum ne carmina manda
> Ne turbata volent rapidis ludibria ventis;
> Ipsa canas, oro.

In H6A:

> The spirit of deep prophecy she hath,
> Exceeding the nine sibyls of old Rome.

Golding says (p. 176a) that the Cumæan Sibyl has the 'spryght of prophesye.' There were commonly held to be ten Sibyls; but they were not all 'of old Rome.' The number nine is doubtless due, as Warburton suggested, to confusion with the *nine* books brought by the Sibyl to Tarquin.

The form 'Sibylla' of Merch. is paralleled in Bacon's *Colors of Good and Evil* 10, and *Advancement of Learning* 2. 23, 33 (Rolfe), and in the Argument to Book 6 of Phaer's Vergil.

Sinon and Wooden Horse.—Lucr. 1501-1561; Hml. 2. 2. 476; Cymb. 3. 4. 61; Tit. 5. 3. 85; H6C 3. 2. 190; Per. 1. 4. 93.

Lucrece finds the story of Sinon pictured in a painting of the fall of Troy, and finds in his falseness a parallel to the

falseness of Tarquin.   The account she gives of the picture
corresponds closely with *Æn.* 2. 13-267.   Thus he is brought
in bound by Phrygian shepherds, and it is Priam who receives
him kindly; cf. *Æn.* 2. 57, 146.   In the remaining passages
we have mere allusions.   In Cymb. his weeping is mentioned; cf. *Æn.* 2. 145.

That Shakespeare read this passage of *Æn.* in the original,
and not in Phaer, is shown by the use of the word Phrygian
in Lucr. 1502.   Cf. *Æn.* 2. 68:

> Constitit atque oculis Phrygia agmina circumspexit.

Phaer omits the name Phrygian.

Sirens.—Err. 3. 2. 47; Mids. 2. 1. 150; Sonn. 119. 1; Tit. 2. 1. 23.
   (Mermaid = Siren) Ven. 429; 777; Lucr. 1411; Err. 3. 2. 45;
   Hml. 4. 7. 177; Ant. 2. 2. 212, 214 (?); H6C 3. 2. 186.

The Sirens who seek to entrap Odysseus by their clear
song in *Od.* 12. 166 seq. have the form of fair women, and
later tradition represents them as half women and half birds;
but in mediæval England they had become identified with
the mermaids of the northern mythology.   Thus Gower, in
Conf. Am. 1. 58, describes a Siren as having the tail of a
fish, and in Chaucer, mermaid is the regular word for Siren:

> Swich swete song was hem among,
> That me thoughte it no briddes song,
> But it was wonder lyk to be
> Song of mermaydens of the see;
> That, for her singing is so clere,
> Though we mermaydens clepe hem here
> In English, as in our usaunce,
> Men clepen hem sereyns in Fraunce.
> *Romaunt of the Rose* 677-684.

Cf. also *Nonne Preestes Tale* 450.   To Shakespeare, then,
the two terms are interchangeable, as for example in Err.,
where both appear.   In most of the passages cited above
Shakespeare is alluding to the song of the Siren or mermaid,
and for this it is not necessary to assign a definite source.
By an obvious metaphor, Siren came to mean harlot, as in

Horace, *Sat.* 2. 3. 14, and in this sense, perhaps, Shakespeare uses the word in Sonn. 199. 1, and probably also in Tit. Less classical and more Teutonic is the reference to the golden hair of the Sirens in Err.:

> Spread o'er the silver waves thy golden hairs.

One is of course reminded of Heine's *Lorelei,* but in *Met.* 13. 738 the sea-nymph, Galatea, is found combing her locks.

Of more difficulty is the apparent reference to 'Siren's tears' in Sonn. 119:

> What potions have I drunk of Siren tears;

and in Err.:

> O, train me not, sweet mermaid, with thy note,
> To drown me in thy sister's flood of tears.

Classical literature furnishes no parallel; nor have I been able to find any in the mermaid-stories of folk-lore. Only in the *Bestiaire* of Philippe de Thaun have I found any mention of tears. Cf. ll. 1361-64:

> Serena en mer hante,
> Cuntre tempeste chante
> E plure en bel tens,
> Itels est sis talenz.

Farther on Philippe explains that the Sirens signify 'Les richeises del munt': they weep

> Quant om dune richeise
> E pur Dé la depreise.

Of course Shakespeare did not know Philippe. The line in Sonn. is probably to be explained by comparison with Psalm 80. 5: 'Thou feedest them with the bread of tears; and givest them tears to drink in great measure.' 'Siren tears' may mean 'deceptive tears'; but the meaning is not clear. In Err. the tears may be explained by the fact that Luciana's sister has really been weeping.

Professor Cook has pointed out the fact that Mids. 2. 1. 150 ff. closely resembles a passage in Ariosto, *Orlando* 6. See

Academy, 30 Nov., 1889. As bearing on this latter passage it is to be noticed that Thetis rides on a dolphin's back in *Met.* 11, Golding, p. 143a and b. Cf. also Golding, p. 17a, where sea-nymphs ride on the backs of fishes.

Sphinx.—LLL 4. 3. 342.

'Subtle as Sphinx.' The monster Sphinx proposed a riddle to all whom she met; when they failed to solve the riddle, she murdered them. Œdipus finally guessed the riddle, upon which the Sphinx killed herself. The familiar story is alluded to by Ovid in *Ibis* 375-376.

Styx.—See Hades.

Sun-Divinities.

Under the name of Phœbus, or Titan, or Hyperion, or without special name, Shakespeare personifies the sun. Usually the personification is not elaborate, though the dark-skinned Cleopatra is 'with Phœbus' amorous pinches black,' Ant. 1. 5. 28; and a woman exposed to the sun 'commits her nicely-gawded cheeks to the wanton spoil of Phœbus' burning kisses,' Cor. 2. 1. 234. Similarly in Cymb. 3. 4. 166 we read: 'exposing it (a cheek) to the greedy touch of common-kissing Titan,' as a parallel to which Steevens quotes from Sidney's *Arcadia:* '. . . and beautifull might have been, if they had not suffered greedy Phœbus, over-often and hard, to kisse them.'

The terms *Phœbus* and *Titan* are used interchangeably, save that Titan is only once spoken of as driving a chariot, Rom. 2. 3. 4; while in nine places Phœbus' chariot is mentioned: Mids. 1. 2. 37; Rom. 3. 2. 2; Ado 5. 3. 26; Hml. 3. 2. 165; Ant. 4. 8. 29; Cymb. 2. 3. 22; Tp. 4. 1. 30; Cymb. 5. 5. 190; H6C 2. 6. 11; and in five passages the car of the sun is mentioned without mythological name: R3. 5. 3. 19; H4A 3. 1. 221; Alls 2. 1. 164; Tit. 2. 1. 5; H6C 4. 7. 80. Twice, Ant. 4. 8. 29; Cymb. 5. 5. 190, the car is spoken of as 'carbuncled' (the palace of the sun is beset with car-buncles in Ovid, Golding, p. 17a).

The treatment of *Hyperion* is somewhat different. In Troil. 2. 3. 207; Tit. 5. 2. 56, he is merely the sun. In H5. 4. 1. 290 a man rising at daybreak is said to 'rise and help Hyperion to his horse,' which suggests a mounted horseman rather than the driver of a chariot. He is twice mentioned in Hml. as a type of beauty: Hamlet's father was to the present king as 'Hyperion to a satyr' (1. 2. 140); and in 3. 4. 56 there is mention of 'Hyperion's curls.' This would seem to indicate that Shakespeare identifies Hyperion with 'flavus Apollo.' Properly Hyperion is not the sun, but a Titan, the father of Helios; but Homer uses the name in a patronymic sense applied to Helios himself (*Od.* 1. 8; 12. 132; *Il.* 8. 480), and later poets follow him, e. g. *Met.* 15. 406; 8. 565. (It may be noticed in passing that Shakespeare falsely accents the word on the antepenultimate.)

Tantalus.—Ven. 599.

> That worse than Tantalus' is her annoy,
> To clip Elysium and to lack her joy.

The suffering of Tantalus is described in *Od.* 11. 582 seq. Though not found in Vergil, and only alluded to by Ovid (*Met.* 4. 458), the idea is none the less a commonplace in modern poetry.

Tartarus.—See Hades.

Telamon.—Ant. 4. 13. 2. See Ajax.

Tellus.—Hml. 3. 2. 166; Per. 4. 1. 14.

Tellus is a mere personification of the earth by its Latin name. In Hml. we have the phrase 'Tellus' orbed ground'; in Per. the name is used as equivalent to earth. Shakespeare may have remembered that in North's Plutarch, *Brutus,* p. 265, there is mention of a temple to 'the goddess Tellus, to wit the earth.'

Tereus.—See Philomel.

Thersites.—Cymb. 4. 2. 252; Troil. passim.

In Cymb. Thersites is a mere type of worthlessness, contrasted with Ajax as a type of manly valor. Apparently Shakespeare has his own Thersites in mind. The foulmouthed railer and coward of Troil. is pretty certainly to be attributed to Homer, *Il.* 2. 211-271, though a hint as to his character might have been learned from *Met.* 13. 233-34:

> At ausus erat reges incessere dictis
> Thersites, etiam per me haud impune, protervis.

Since Shakespeare gives to him many of the attributes of his clowns, it may be significant that Chapman calls him 'jester.'

Theseus.

The slight sketch of Theseus, Duke of Athens, as we have it in Mids., is to be traced to Plutarch's life of Theseus in North's translation. Chaucer in the *Knightes Tale* mentions the marriage of Theseus and Ipolita, but does not give the names of Theseus's former loves, Perigenia, Ægle, and Antiopa (Mids. 2. 1. 78-80). These are given by North on pp. 41, 57, 68 (Temple ed.), though the name Perigenia appears as Perigouna. Shakespeare's spelling, Hippolyta, is also that of North. That she is an Amazon against whom Theseus has been making war is mentioned by North on pp. 70-71. That Theseus is a kinsman of Hercules (Mids. 5. 1. 47) is provided for by North on p. 40. For Hippolyta's statement (Mids. 4. 1. 116)—

> I was with Hercules and Cadmus once,
> When in a wood of Crete they bay'd the bear
> With hounds of Sparta—

I find no authority either in Chaucer or North. Theseus is mentioned also in Gent. 4. 4. 173 (see Ariadne).

Thetis.—Troil. 1. 3. 39; Ant. 3. 7. 61; Per. 4. 4. 39.

In Troil. and in Per. Thetis is merely a personification of the sea. In Ant., Antony calls Cleopatra his Thetis, probably, as Malone suggests, alluding to her voyage down the Cydnus.

Thetis is represented by Homer as sitting 'in the sea-depths beside her aged sire,' *Il.* 1. 358, etc. Ovid speaks of her as 'numen aquarum,' *Am.* 2. 14. 14. See also *Met.* 11. 221 seq. Her name is used by metonymy for the sea only in later Latin authors. Cf. Martial 10. 13. 4, and Claudian, *Rapt. Pros.* 1. 148; but Tethys is so used in *Met.* 2. 69, 509. May Shakespeare have confused the two?

Thisbe.—See Pyramus.

Titan.—See Sun-divinities.

Titania.

The name given by Shakespeare to the queen of fairies in Mids. See Diana.

Tityus (?).—H4B 5. 3. 146; Wiv. 1. 3. 94; Lr. 2. 4. 137; Tit. 5. 2. 31; H6A 4. 3. 47.

Tityus is never mentioned by name in Shakespeare, but in the passages cited above the references to a vulture tearing at the vitals seem to suggest the fate of Tityus as described in *Æn.* 6. 595-600 and *Met.* 4. 457. Perhaps they should rather be referred to Prometheus. Two of the speeches are spoken by Pistol.

Triton.—Cor. 3. 1. 89.

Coriolanus calls Sicinius a 'Triton of the minnows,' and a few lines farther on speaks of 'the horn and noise of the monster.' Triton is described in *Met.* 1. 333.

Troilus and Cressida.—Merch. 5. 1. 4; Wiv. 1. 3. 83; H5. 2. 1. 80; Ado 5. 2. 31; As 4. 1. 97; Tw. 3. 1. 59; Alls 2. 1. 100; Troil. passim.

It will be noticed at once that all these allusions outside of Troil. range within five years, 1596-1601, and that all but the first come between 1599-1601. In Ado and As, Troilus alone is mentioned (humorously) as a 'pattern of love.' In the second of these instances Rosalind says: 'Troilus had his brains dashed out with a Grecian club.' This is not

related by Chaucer, but Caxton gives the following account
(p. 639) : 'Then cam on Achilles whan he sawe troilus alle
naked (i. e. deprived of his armor) And ran upon hym in a
rage And smote of his heed And cast it under the feet of the
horse And toke the body and bonde it to the taylle of his
horse And so drewe hit after hym thurgh oute the ooste.'
In Wiv., Tw., and Alls, Pandarus is the point of allusion,
which in each case is playful. The only serious reference
is in Merch.:

> The moon shines bright: in such a night as this,
> Troilus methinks mounted the Troyan walls
> And sigh'd his soul toward the Grecian tents,
> Where Cressid lay that night,

which is closely copied from Chaucer's *Troylus* 5. 648, 666.

The source of the Troilus story in Troil. is to be found
in Chaucer. I shall not attempt to notice the changes Shake-
peare has introduced. See Stache, *Das Verhältniss von
Shakespeares Troilus and Cressida zu Chaucers gleich-
namigen Gedicht,* Nordhausen, 1893, and R. A. Small,
Stage-Quarrel, pp. 154-156.

Troilus is mentioned as swounding in battle in the Troy-
picture in Lucr. 1486. A disparaging allusion to Cressid is
made by Pistol in H5. 2. 1. 80.

Typhon.—Troil. 1. 3. 160; Tit. 4. 2. 94.

The name Typhon is used by Shakespeare rather indefinitely
for 'giant.' Typhoeus was one of the giants who warred
against the gods, *Met.* 5. 321. In this passage Golding
substitutes 'Typhon' (p. 69a). The two names, originally
distinct, had already become confused among the ancients.

Ulysses.—Lucr. 1399; Cor. 1. 3. 93; H6C 3. 2. 189; 4. 2. 19; Troil.
passim.

Caxton characterizes Ulysses as 'the moste fayr man among
all the grekes/ But he was deceyvable And subtyll. And
sayd his thynges Ioyously. He was a right grete lyar And
was so well bespoken that he had none felawe ne like to

8

hym' (p. 541). From *Met.* 13, also, where Ulysses disputes with Ajax over the arms of Achilles, we get a similar
notion of his character, which is both in Caxton and Ovid a
natural development of Homer's 'Odysseus of many counsels.'

In the Troy-painting in Lucr. he is depicted near Ajax:

> But the mild glance that sly Ulysses lent
> Show'd deep regard and smiling government.

The phrase 'sly Ulysses' occurs several times in Golding (pp.
160b, 167a) where the original shows no equivalent. It was
apparently his stock epithet in Shakespeare's time. The
'mild glance' suggests Golding, p. 162a (*Met.* 13. 125):

> (He) raysed soberly his eyliddes from the ground
> On which he had a little whyle them pitched in a stound.

In H6C 3. he is again a type of sly deceit. In Act 4 of the
same play we have a reference to the capture of Rhesus'
steeds:

> That as Ulysses and stout Diomede
> With sleight and manhood stole to Rhesus' tents,
> And brought from thence the Thracian fatal steeds.

This exploit is described at length in *Iliad* 10, and forms the
subject of one of Euripides' dramas, and is several times
alluded to in Ovid (*Art.* 2. 137; *Met.* 13. 249); but none of
these authorities explain the word fatal. In his comment
on *Æn.* 1. 469, Servius, however, explains: 'quibus pende-
bant fata Troiana; ut si pabulo Troiano usi essent vel e
Xantho Troiæ fluvio bibissent, Troia perire non posset.'

Penelope and the yarn spun in Ulysses' absence are mentioned in Cor. 1. 3. 92. The ultimate source is of course
Odyssey 19. 149 seq., but the story is mentioned in *Her.* 1. 10
(from which Shakespeare quotes in Shr.). For so familiar
an incident it is impossible to name a definite source.

The character of Ulysses in Troil. presents no divergences
from the conception stated above. Cf. Ajax.

Venus.

The conception of Venus shown in Shakespeare's earliest
production, *Venus and Adonis,* that of goddess of lust rather

than of love, is the usual conception in the dramas. A line from Golding's Preface to his Ovid (p. 1b) shows that the conception is not peculiar to Shakespeare; we are told to understand

By Venus such as of the fleshe too filthie lust are bent.

Of the nobler Greek conception of Aphrodite there is no hint, nor is there mention of her birth from the sea-foam.

Venus is mentioned by name 23 times, exclusive of Ven.; as Cytherea 5 times; and as Love (followed by feminine pronoun) 6 times. Save for the five occurrences in Troil., these mentions are largely in the earlier plays, only seven coming later than 1600 (Ant. 3 times, Tp. once, Cymb. twice, Wint. once).

Of the attributes of Venus, her doves are mentioned seven times: Ven. 153; 1190; Mids. 1. 1. 171; Lucr. 58; Rom. 2. 5. 7; Merch. 2. 6. 5 ('pigeons'); Tp. 4. 1. 94. In the last of these passages she is 'cutting the clouds towards Paphos, and her son dove-drawn with her.' (Cf. also Per. 4. Ind. 32.) The doves are frequently mentioned by Ovid, e. g. *Met.* 14. 597. Their significance is explained in Rom. 2. 5. 7. Paphos is mentioned in the story of Venus and Adonis, *Met.* 10. 530. She is mentioned as mother of Cupid in Tp. (v. *supra*) and in LLL 2. 1. 254. She is several times a type of beauty: Troil. 3. 1. 34; Ant. 2. 2. 205; Cymb. 2. 2. 14; 5. 5. 164; Wint. 4. 4. 122 (i. e. in later plays). At times she is confused with the star named after her, either with or without astrological significance: Mids. 3. 2. 61; 3. 2. 107; H4B 2. 4. 268; Tit. 2. 3. 30; H6A 1. 2. 144. As an astrological influence she is opposed to Saturn.

Most serious and noble of the allusions to Venus is that in Mids. 1. 1. 171 where Hermia swears to Lysander,

By the simplicity of Venus' doves,
By that which knitteth souls and prospers loves.

In the latter line Furness sees an allusion to the cestus of Venus. Shakespeare might have read of it in Martial 6. 13, but it is more fully described in *Iliad* 14. 214, 'the embroidered girdle, fair-wrought, wherein are all enchantments; therein are love, and desire, and loving converse, that steals the wits even of the wise.'

For Venus in her relations to Adonis, Mars, Vulcan, Anchises, see under those heads.

Love is frequently personified without demonstrable reference to either Cupid or Venus. A notable example is LLL 4. 3. 344:

> And when Love speaks, the voice of all the gods
> Make heaven drowsy with the harmony.

Vulcan.—Ado 1. 1. 187; Tw. 5. 1. 56; Hml. 3. 2. 89. Troil. 1. 3. 168; 5. 2. 170; Tit. 2. 1. 89.

Shakespeare knows Vulcan as the blacksmith divinity, forging armor in the depths of the earth (Troil. 5), a conception which may be traced to *Æn.* 8. 407-453 or *Iliad* 18 369 seq. His grimy face is alluded to in Tw. and in Hml.:

> If his (the king's) occulted guilt
> Do not itself unkennel in one speech,
> It is a damned ghost that we have seen,
> And my imaginations are as foul
> As Vulcan's stithy;

of which Delius says: 'The connection of thought between Vulcan's realm and the Christian hell whence the "damned ghost" issues is very common among Shakespeare's contemporaries.'

In Troil. 1. 3. 168: 'As like as Vulcan and his wife,' i. e. *unlike.* We are told by Ovid in *Art.* 2. 569 that Venus used often to amuse Mars by imitating her husband's awkward manners. He is alluded to as a type of cuckold in Tit. (see Mars).

PART SECOND

THE MYTHOLOGY OF THE SEVERAL WORKS

(The plays and poems are treated in what the author believes to be the approximate chronological order.)

Venus and Adonis.

The story of Venus and Adonis as told by Shakespeare is a combination of two Ovidian stories (see s. v. Adonis); but of Ovidian allusions in the course of the poem we have but 2—a reference to Narcissus, and one to the intrigue of Mars and Venus. Cupid is mentioned once by name, and twice by implication. There are 4 allusions to the divinities as nature-personifications. A reference to Tantalus and Elysium is the only possible Vergilian indebtedness.

Love's Labor's Lost.

Critics are substantially agreed in considering LLL Shakespeare's earliest independent drama, but the probability that it received a considerable revision in 1598 makes it unsafe to use the play as a basis for any generalization as to the poet's treatment of mythology in his earliest period. The numerous allusions of a playful or humorous character, especially in the speeches of Biron, suggest the manner of such plays as Ado or As rather than that of the earlier works.

The play contains 38 mythological allusions (+ an oath by Jove, and numerous mentions of Hector, who appears as one of the Nine Worthies); but, although the allusions are numerous and varied, they are neither very definite nor very artistic. Cupid is mentioned 10 times, always playfully, Venus twice, and Love twice. Jove is twice referred to in erotic connection, and in one of these instances Juno is mentioned with him. Nature-nymph appears but once in a

pedantic speech of Holofernes.   Other divinities mentioned
are: Bacchus, Mercury as orator, Apollo as patron of
music, Mars.   Of the 8 allusions to mythological matter
contained in Ovid, 6 are to Hercules, and only one, a reference to Argus, is at all definite.   There is no suggestion of
Vergilian influence, though several heroes of the Trojan
war are mentioned incidentally.   Eighteen of theytholog-
ical allusions are in speeches of Biron.

Comedy of Errors.

Though Err. is modeled on a classical original, classical
mythology appears but little in its dialogue.   There are
only 6 mythological allusions, 2 of them humorous.

Two Gentlemen of Verona.

Of the 8 mythological allusions in Gent., 5 are definite,
and 3 vague.   Of the former, 2 are to Hero and Leander,
and the remaining 3 to Ovidian fable.   Though neither
Cupid nor Venus is mentioned by name, there are 12 mentions of Love with attributes of Cupid (or Venus).   ᾽Nature-
myth is represented only in an oath by the 'pale queen of
night.'   Save in an oath by Jove, the gods do not appear at
all; nor is the Trojan war ever alluded to.   The allusions
all occur in speeches of the serious characters.   The date
of Gent. is very uncertain; it has been placed as early as
1590, and as late as 1595.   The relatively large proportion
of Ovidian allusions would lead us to place it near Merch.,
while the small number of the allusions, and the total
absence of the divinities, suggest the manner of Err.

The Rape of Lucrece.

Though the date of Lucr. is uncertain, its publication in
1594 and the general character of its composition lead the
critics to assign it to about the same period as Gent., an
assignation which is borne out by an examination of the
mythology of the two pieces.   The mythology in Lucr. is
largely confined to the elaborate description of the painting

in the house of Lucrece, depicting scenes from the Trojan war, a description which shows evident familiarity with *Æn.* 2.   Ovidian story is represented by 4 allusions.   A personification of night is the only instance of nature-myth, while an appeal to 'high almighty Jove,' and a reference to the doves of Venus, are the only mentions of the divinities.

King Richard II.

R2 contains 6 mythological allusions: one to Neptune as the sea, 2 to Mars as god of war, one to the shears of destiny, one to Troy, and one of Ovidian origin to 'glistering Phaeton,' who 'wanted the manage of unruly jades.'   This last is the only definite allusion.   The paucity of mythological allusion in this and the two histories belonging to the same period is to be explained in part at least by the character of their subjects.   Among scenes of battle and murder the graceful stories of Ovid seem out of place.   The single Ovidian allusion is spoken by the poetical Richard.

King Richard III.

Of the 5 mythological allusions in R3, 2 are to Mercury as the winged messenger of Jove, one to the chariot of the sun, one to Lethe as the river of forgetfulness, and one an elaborate reference to the Vergilian Hades.

King John.

There are 8 mythological allusions in K. J., distributed one each among the following subjects: Neptune as the sea, Mars as the god of war, Mercury as the messenger, Ate as spirit of discord, Hercules, the Amazons, Rumor, the shears of Destiny.   None of the allusions is at all definite, and none is to Ovidian story nor to the Trojan war.

Merchant of Venice.

Though several plays have a larger number of allusions than Merch., in none is mythology employed with greater appropriateness and beauty.   Of the 28 mythological allusions, 13 are detailed, and several are highly elaborate. Of these detailed allusions, 10 are to Ovidian story. To Medea and Jason there are 3 separate allusions, though the myth is no where else referred to in the authentic plays. Nature-myth appears twice. Cupid is twice mentioned, and other divinities 5 times. It is to be noticed that mythological allusion is entirely absent from the serious scenes of Act 4 (the trial), but that it is especially frequent in the garden scene of Act 5. Except for 3 humorous allusions spoken by Launcelot Gobbo, the mythology is confined to the high comedy characters. It is introduced mainly as simile or metaphor. Merch. should probably be attributed to 1594-1596, though the date is very uncertain.

Midsummer Night's Dream.

There are 37 mythological allusions in Mids., exclusive of references to Theseus, who is one of the characters of the play. (Pyramus and Thisbe is counted as one allusion.) The influence of Ovid, though much less than in Merch., is yet rather strong; there are 5 references to definite Ovidian myth, and in five or six other allusions Ovid's influence may be discovered. Of Vergil there is but slight trace, and a single reference to Helen's beauty is the only hint of the Trojan war. The number of nature-myths is noticeable; 8 such personifications occur in the play. Of other divinities, Diana is twice mentioned as patroness of chastity, and Venus 3 times as goddess of love, rather than of lust as usually in Shakespeare. Cupid is named in 6 passages with more seriousness than in any other play.

If we divide the 37 allusions in the play among the three sets of characters composing the *dramatis personæ*, we find that 15 fall to the high comedy characters, 10 to the mechanicals and their play of Pyramus and Thisbe, and the remaining 12 to the fairy personages. In this latter group fall 5 of the 8 nature-myths, and many of the most delicate and beautiful allusions of the play. The fairies speak of Hecate's team and of Cupid as objects of their own experience, and in general use mythology with great appropriateness. The mechanicals, of course, bungle their mythology terribly, giving us 'Shefalus and Procrus,' 'Helen and Limander,' 'Phibbus' car,' and 'Ercles.'

Romeo and Juliet.

Of the 25 mythological allusions in Rom., 4 are to nature-myths connected with the sun or moon, 3 to Venus as goddess of love, 10 to Cupid—when his name is mentioned the allusion is always playful, but Love with attributes of Cupid is treated more seriously—2 to Diana as patroness of chastity. Of distinctly Ovidian origin are the references to the cave of Echo and to Phaeton. Playful mentions of Dido and of Helen as types of beauty constitute the only allusions to Vergil or to the Trojan war. All but 5 of the allusions in Rom. occur in the first two acts. This absence of mythological allusion in the closing acts explains the comparative paucity of the allusions. It is generally admitted that Rom. received its final form in 1595–1596, though a first draft may have been written as early as 1591.

King Henry IV, Part I.

The 12 mythological allusions in H4A do not differ greatly in subject matter from those of the earlier histories. Mars (2) as war-god, and Minerva (?) in the same capacity, Mercury, Hydra, and the chariot of the sun are mentioned by the serious characters; Falstaff, in a speech of delicate humor, mentions Diana in her double capacity as goddess of the moon and of the chase, speaks of Phœbus and Titan as sun-divinities, and compares his valor to that of Hercules; but there are no instances of ridiculous allusion such as are to be found in the speeches of Pistol in H4B. The play may safely be assigned to 1596 or 1597.

King Henry IV, Part II.

Beginning with H4B we have a group of plays in which the mythological allusion assumes a playful, humorous,

or even farcical character. Of the playful or humorous
treatment Wiv., Ado, and As offer the best examples; of
the farcical treatment the best instance is furnished by the
ranting speeches of Pistol in the present play. In considering the mythology of H4B, it is necessary to separate this
mass of ridiculous allusion, spoken by Pistol and the other
tavern-frequenters, from the allusions of the serious personages. The mythology of the blank-verse characters is like
that of the other histories. There are 7 such references,
distributed as follows: Rumor (2) (she appears once on
the stage dressed like Vergil's Fama), Neptune as the sea,
Mars (2) as war-god, Lethe as the river of forgetfulness,
Hydra (probable contamination with the Argus-myth), and
one allusion to Priam and the fall of Troy, which indicates
direct borrowing from *Æn.* 2 (see s. v. Priam). In the
speeches of Pistol mythological allusion is continual and
absurd. Though it is impossible to trace many of his allusions, they seem in the main to be Vergilian rather than
Ovidian; Pistol is especially fond of the mythology of the
infernal regions. Six allusions are made by the other prose
characters, among which we find two references of Ovidian
origin. H4B may be dated 1598.

Merry Wives of Windsor.

The 12 mythological allusions in Wiv. are all more or
less humorous. Four of them are spoken by Pistol. Of
distinctly Ovidian source are Mrs. Page's allusion to the
giants buried under Mount Pelion, Falstaff's elaborate reference to Jove and Europa, and the two mentions of Actæon.
The total absence of nature-myth is to be remarked. Wiv.
was written in 1599, directly after H4B.

King Henry V.

H5 furnishes a contrast to the other plays of the same
period in the greater seriousness of its mythology. Of the
18 allusions, only one, a reference by Pistol to Parca's fatal
web, is of a humorous nature. Of ultimate Ovidian origin

are an erroneous reference to Perseus and Pegasus and a mention of the pipe of Hermes, both in a speech by the Dauphin.   Mars appears twice as god of war, and the winged Mercury is once mentioned.   Of nature-myth we find 4 instances.   H5 was written in 1599.

Much Ado About Nothing.

The mythology of Ado is overwhelmingly humorous in its character.   Of the 30 allusions, 25 are playful, and of the remaining 5, three occur in passages of rimed verse. There are 10 references to Cupid, all playful.   Nature-myth occurs twice.   Diana appears twice as patroness of chastity, Venus once as goddess of lust, and Vulcan as carpenter. There are but 2 distinctly Ovidian allusions—to the story of Philemon and Baucis and to Europa.   Twelve of the allusions are spoken by Benedick, and two by Beatrice. Date, 1599.

As You Like It.

The more poetical character of As and Tw. explains the greater seriousness of the mythological allusion in these plays as compared with Ado.   Of the 27 allusions in As only 13 are humorous.   For the same reason, perhaps, the influence of Ovid asserts itself strongly again in As.   There are 7 instances of direct Ovidian allusion, while 4 other passages are suggestive of Ovid's influence.   Of these 11 Ovidian passages, only 3 are humorous.   Nature-myth appears only once, where Diana is addressed as thrice-crowned queen of night' in a love-poem of Orlando.   Of the divinities representing ethical qualities, we have Diana twice as a type of chastity and Cupid 4 times as love-god— he is mentioned twice by name and twice by implication, once seriously in a speech by the pastoral Silvius; Juno is patroness of marriage, and Hymen appears on the stage in the same capacity.   There are two Troy-allusions—to Helen and to Troilus.   Date, 1600.

Twelfth Night.

If we except numerous mentions of Jove (= God) in speeches of Malvolio and Feste, there remain 15 mythological allusions in Tw. Of these, 7 are of the playful sort so common in the other plays of the same period, but the remaining 8 are allusions of a peculiar grace and appropriateness. Such is the Duke's veiled allusion to Actæon in the lines:

> That instant was I turn'd into a hart;
> And my desires, like fell and cruel hounds,
> E'er since pursue me.

So, too, his reference to the 'rich golden shaft' of love. Still another graceful Ovidian allusion is the sea-captain's comparison of Sebastian bound to the mast with Arion on the dolphin's back. Mercury appears as the inspirer of lying, Vulcan as the blacksmith, and Diana as the tender maiden; probably Saturn is the 'melancholy god' referred to by Feste in 2. 4. 75. These are the only mentions of the greater divinities; nature-myth does not occur at all. Humorous mentions of Troilus and Cressida, Penthesilea, and the Myrmidons constitute the only Troy-allusions. The play was written in 1601.

All's Well That Ends Well.

The date of Alls is very uncertain; Lee, on the assumption that it is the 'Love's Labors Won' mentioned by Meres, assigns it to 1595; Gollancz believes that it was first written in 1590-92, and revised in 1602. Perhaps the majority of critics would assign it to the same period as Hml.—somewhere between 1601 and 1602; and the mythology of the play would tend to support such an assignment. Of the 25 mythological allusions, few are more than mere conventional references. Seven of them, spoken by the boasting coward Parolles, suggest the manner of the preceding comedies; while the paucity of Ovidian allusion, and the more frequent mention of the divinities, connect the play with Hml. and the dramas which follow. The nature-mythology is confined to single mentions of Iris as the rainbow, Hesperus, and the horses of the sun; Diana appears 3 times as patroness of chastity, Cupid is twice mentioned playfully, and Plutus appears as god of riches. There are but 2 Ovidian allusions. Of Troy-allusions we have humorous references to Pandar, and to Helen as the cause of the Trojan war.

Troilus and Cressida.

The mythology of Troil. is discussed at length in the Introduction, pp. 17-19.

The Sonnets.

Without attempting to pronounce on the date of the Sonnets, I have followed Furnivall's order, and considered them as belonging to this general period. They contain but 10 mythological allusions, of which none is of much significance. Cupid appears 3 times; Diana, Mars, and Saturn once each. The only trace of Ovidian myth is in an allusion to Adonis. There is no instance of nature-myth.

Hamlet.

In considering the mythology of Hml., it is necessary to distinguish between the speeches of the players in the 'Mouse Trap' and the long account of Priam's death, and the speeches of the regular characters of the drama. If, then, we except the speeches of the players, we find 19 mythological allusions, of which 14 are spoken by Hamlet himself. Hamlet is a scholar and a thinker, so that the frequency of his classical allusion is in perfect accord with his character. Serious use of nature-myth occurs three times in speeches of the scholar, Horatio.

Turning now to the speeches of the players, we find first a long account of the fall of Troy, certainly to be referred to *Æn.* 2 (see s. v. Priam), and in the course of the speech another direct Vergilian allusion in the mention of the Cyclops as forging armor for Mars. In the 'Mouse Trap' we find conventional allusions to Neptune, Tellus, the car of Phœbus, Hymen, and Hecate. Except for the mention of Tellus, there is nothing in the mythology of the players' speeches to cast doubt on their Shakespearian authorship.

Considering the play as a whole, one is impressed by the paucity of Ovidian reference, and by the relatively frequent traces of Vergil's influence. Hml. was probably written in 1601–1602. (See further what is said of the mythology of the play in the Introduction, p. 9.)

Julius Cæsar.

The mythology of Cæs. consists of only 5 allusions, of which one is to Æneas and Anchises, one to Erebus, one to Ate, and 2 to Olympus, with a possible sixth allusion to Deucalion's flood. This absence of mythology is in keeping with the studied severity of style in which the play is conceived and executed. Cæs. was certainly written in 1601.

Measure for Measure.

In Meas. Shakespeare's mythological allusion reaches its lowest ebb. There are but 2 allusions—one to Jove as the thunderer, spoken by Isabel, and a humorous reference to the myth of Pygmalion's image, spoken by Lucio. The play is usually assigned to 1604.

Othello.

There are 11 mythological allusions in Oth., of which 6 are in speeches of Othello himself. Written in 1604. (See further what is said of this play in the Introduction, p. 12.)

Macbeth.

There are but 8 mythological allusions in Mcb., and of these all but one are to the more terrible or destructive elements of ancient religion. There is one instance of nature-myth in a mention of Neptune. Neither Ovidian myth nor the Trojan war receives any mention. All the allusions occur in speeches of Macbeth, Lady Macbeth, or the witches. Written in 1604-1606. (See further in Introduction, p. 12.)

King Lear.

Besides oaths by Juno, Jove, Apollo, and Hecate, which Shakespeare introduces to indicate the pagan setting of the play, there are 5 clear mythological allusions in Lr., and 2 probable allusions *tacito nomine.* Lear himself appeals to 'high-judging Jove,' 'the thunder-bearer,' uses the Centaur as a type of human nature, half man, half beast, and in grim mad humor calls the eyeless Gloucester 'blind Cupid.' Of his own suffering he speaks in words which seem to suggest the punishments of Ixion and of Tityus. Kent, in a mocking speech, speaks of 'flickering Phœbus' front'; and, overcome by the trickery of Oswald, compares himself to blunt Ajax cozened by the false Ulysses. This last is the only distinct Ovidian allusion in the play. Lr. is to be assigned to 1605.

Timon of Athens.

Though Tim. is commonly attributed to 1607-1608, the date is so uncertain that I feel justified in assigning it on mythological grounds to the period of Mcb. and Lr., rather than to that of Cor. and Cymb. Both in the number and the character of its mythological allusions it serves as a bridge between the paucity of allusion in Lr. and the abundant allusion of Ant. The 11 mythological allusions are, with two exceptions, to divinities who personify either the powers of nature or the moral influences in the life of man. In the first of these categories we find mentions of Neptune and Hyperion, and of the moon as sister of the sun. Perhaps, too, the Jove who 'o'er some high-viced city hangs his poison in the sick air' is thought of, in part at least, as divinity of the sky. In the second category are Mars, Diana, Plutus, Cupid, and Hymen. Cupid appears on the stage with a masque of ladies as Amazons. The remaining allusion is to the Phœnix.

It is generally admitted that Tim. is only in part the work of Shakespeare; but the task of dividing the Shakespearian from the non-Shakespearian is a ticklish one. If

9

we may accept provisionally the division given by Gollancz in the preface to the Temple ed., we find that the masque in which Cupid and the ladies appear is not genuine; but that all the other mythological allusions occur in the genuine portions, with possible exception of the allusion to Plutus. With these exceptions, then, the mythology of the play may be thought of as Shakespeare's.

Antony and Cleopatra.

In the series of great tragedies, classical mythology plays a quite insignificant part; but in Ant. and Cor. it suddenly reasserts itself with surprising vigor; from the 7 allusions of Lr. and the 11 of Tim., we jump in Ant. to 39 allusions, covering a considerable range of subject. A chief characteristic of the mythology in plays of this period is the frequent allusion to the greater divinities. Jove appears as supreme god, as thunderer, and as the sender of rain—6 times in all, exclusive of a few colorless allusions occasioned by the pagan setting of the play. Mars is mentioned 3 times, Venus 3 times, and Cupid, Mercury, and Bacchus once each. There are 5 instances of nature-myth. Ovidian myth is represented by 6 allusions. The Troy-story is 4 times alluded to—Hector as a type of bravery, Ajax twice (of Ovidian origin), and Dido and Æneas as famous lovers. The only other evidences of Vergilian influence are in references to Lethe (2), Elysium, and a snake-crowned Fury.

Eleven of the allusions are spoken by Antony, and 10 by Cleopatra; the rest are distributed among a number of characters. The play was probably written in 1607-1608.

Coriolanus.

Of the 26 mythological allusions in Cor., 16 are references to the greater divinities (oaths by Jupiter and Juno are excluded from consideration). Jupiter as supreme god and as thunderer is mentioned 5 times; Juno as a type of anger and jealousy, twice; Mars as god of war or as a type of military valor, 5 times; Phœbus as the sun, Neptune with his trident, Diana as type of chastity, and Pluto as god of the lower world, once each. There are 4 Troy-allusions. The date of Cor. must fall between 1608 and 1610.

Cymbeline.

If we exclude from consideration the elaborate masque in 5. 4, the authenticity of which has been doubted, and the incidental references to Jove which mark the pagan background of the play, we find 31 mythological allusions in Cymb. About 75 per cent. of these allusions have to do with the greater divinities, while the Ovidian allusion consists of single references to the tale of Tereus and to the madness of Hecuba.

In the masque of Act 5, Jove descends in thunder and lightning, credited with many of the attributes of the Hebrew Jehovah, and in the course of the dialogue occur allusions to Lucina and to Elysium. One passage strongly suggests an incident of the *Iliad* to which Shakespeare had already alluded in Troil. (see s. v. Mars). There is nothing in the mythology of this masque to mark it as un-Shakespearian. 1609-1610. (See further in Introduction, p. 13.)

Tempest.

Mythology enters largely into the stage machinery of Tp.; Ariel disguises himself as a water-nymph, and as a Harpy, in the latter disguise snatching away a banquet in a manner evidently suggested by a Vergilian episode; into Act 4 is inserted an elaborate masque, occupying 57 lines, in which Juno, Ceres, Iris, and 'certain nymphs' appear. In the course of this masque we find allusions to the intrigue of Mars and Venus, and to the rape of Proserpina; but these are the only Ovidian stories alluded to in the play, though Prospero's incantation in 4. 1 is indebted to Golding's version of *Met.* 7. Besides the passages referred to above, there are 7 mythological allusions in the play, of which 5 are to nature-divinities. The allusions always occur in speeches of the higher characters. Tp. is generally assigned to 1610–1611.

Winter's Tale.

If we except the frequent references to Apollo, occasioned by the consultation of his oracle—a detail of the plot which Shakespeare took from the novel which forms his main source for the drama—and except also two references to Jove (= God) due to the pagan setting of the play, we have left 13 mythological allusions in Wint. Of these 13 allusions, one, a mention of Jove's thunder, occurs in Act 3; one, a use of Neptune, by metonymy, for the sea, is in Act 5; all the rest fall in Act 4, the act of idyllic love-making and pastoral life. From the stern scenes of the earlier acts mythology is quite excluded. Even within Act 4 the mythology is confined to a few speeches: 4 of the allusions are spoken by Florizel in the course of 30 consecutive lines, and 4 are spoken by Perdita in the course of only 8 lines. The 4 allusions spoken by Florizel are taken over bodily from *Dorastus and Fawnia,* and thus lose much of their significance. They mention transformations of Jupiter, Neptune, and Apollo; for the last divinity Shakespeare has added the epithet 'fire-robed,' and for Neptune the adjective 'green,' thus emphasizing their physical bases. Perdita's charming speech beginning:

> O Proserpina,
> For the flowers now, that frighted thou let'st fall
> From Dis's waggon!

indicates definite acquaintance with Ovid; and the name Autolycus, and the reference to Deucalion, are also of Ovidian origin.

PLAYS OF DOUBTFUL AUTHENTICITY.

Titus Andronicus.

The mythology of Tit. is discussed at length in the Introduction, pp. 15-17.

Henry VI. Pt. I.

H6A contains 18 mythological allusions, of which 4 are to Ovidian material, 4 to the divinities, 4 to the Troy-story. Most of the mythological personages appear as types of some moral quality. Nature-myth does not occur. The treatment of the mythology does not differ essentially from that in the earlier of the authentic plays; but several of the myths alluded to do not appear in the genuine works—such are the allusions to the Minotaur, Icarus, Astræa, Nemesis, and the gardens of Adonis. One may add, too, that the *typical* use of mythology is not usual in Shakespeare till a later period.

Henry VI. Pt. II.

The 13 mythological allusions of H6B resemble those of H6A, save that they appear in formal simile rather than as mere types. Three are to Ovid, 4 to the divinities, and 5 to the Troy-story. Allusions to Medea and Absyrtus, to Iris as messenger rather than as rainbow, to the brazen caves of Æolus, and to the incident of Telephus wounded and cured by the spear of Achilles, find no counterpart in the dramas of unquestioned authenticity.

Henry VI. Pt. III.

Of the 24 allusions in H6C, 10 have to do with the Trojan war, 6 with Ovidian story, and 6 with the divinities, including 2 instances of nature-myth. They are usually introduced in simile. An elaborate allusion to Dædalus and Icarus is strongly suggestive of two similar allusions in H6A. The mention of the 'fatal steeds' of Rhesus, and their capture by Ulysses and Diomede, is distinctly non-Shakespearian.

Taming of the Shrew.

If we could be sure that the play as it stands is merely Shakespeare's working over of the older *Taming of a Shrew,* it would be possible to ascribe to Shakespeare all the mythology of the existing play, for none of the allusions is to be found in the old play; but the probability that the play represents further collaboration makes such an ascription unsafe. The mythology of Shr. is overwhelmingly Ovidian; of the 13 allusions, 9 are to be traced either to *Met.* or to *Her.,* and from *Her.* we have a direct quotation. One allusion only, to Dido and Anna, is of Vergilian origin. There is no instance of nature-myth, and the greater divinities receive but scanty attention. There is nothing either in substance or in treatment to prevent one from assigning the play to about the same period as Merch., in which Ovidian influence is also very strong.

Pericles.

If we except frequent references to Diana, occasioned by the machinery of the play, we find in Per. 25 instances of mythological allusion, of which 15 are in the portion of the drama which may safely be assigned to Shakespeare (the last three acts, with the exception of the brothel scenes in Act 4). We are immediately impressed by the total absence of Ovidian allusion in the authentic portion; while a mention of the Harpies is the only trace of Vergilian influence. As in Cymb. and Wint., the greater divinities are often mentioned, and nature-myth is frequent. Turning to the spurious portions, we find a considerable Ovidian influence—the garden of the Hesperides, Jove as a type of wantonness, and Priapus. Cupid is also mentioned.

Henry VIII.

The mythology of H8 is confined to a charming song of twelve lines about Orpheus and his lute, and a reference to the Phœnix.

PR
3009
.R72
.

c. 2

CITY COLLEGE LIBRARY
1825 MAY ST.
BROWNSVILLE, TEXAS 78520

PR
3009
.R72

    Root, Robert Kilburn, 1877—1950.
      Classical mythology in Shake-
speare. New York, Gordian Press,
1965.
      134 p. 23 cm. (Yale studies in
English, 19)

      1. Shakespeare, William, 1564—
1616—Folklore, mythology. I.
Title.   (Series)

PR3009.R72   822.33

                                   65—24

0 50 97   07   758469   © THE BAKER & TAYLOR CO. 8